Design in Sweden

THE SWEDISH INSTITUTE

in collaboration with

THE SWEDISH SOCIETY OF INDUSTRIAL DESIGN

CONTENTS

Photographers: Karl-Olov Bergström, Björn G Breitholz, Bengt Carlén, Bengt-Göran Carlsson, Björn Enström, Bengt af Geijerstam/BILD-HUSET, Hans Hammarskiöld/TIOFOTO, Christer Hallgren, Håkan Johansson, Stefan Lindberg, Jean Montgrenier, Nelanders Foto, Leif O Pehrson, Lars Rosengren, Reijo Rüster, Carl Johan Rönn, Rolf Salomonsson, Sune Sundahl, Gunnar Wallin, Ove Wallin, Gunnar Wåhlén.

Editor: Lennart Lindkvist
© The Swedish Institute
The authors are solely responsible for the opinions expressed in this book.
Design by Vidar Forsberg
Translated by Claude Stephenson
Cover: "Jaguar," glass plate by Paul Hoff, Kosta-Boda
Printed in Sweden by
AB Tryckerigruppen, Malmö 1977
ISBN 91-520-0069-9

The new edition of *Design in Sweden*, now appearing after five years, is largely a new book. This is true not only of its appearance, a new format and new layout, but also of its contents, which have been re-worked and brought up to date, with some chapters being completely rewritten. The authors look back at Swedish art handicrafts and indus-trial design during the 1950s and 1960s, summarize what has happened during the 1970s and report on the current situation for Swedish design.

Today's situation is complicated, difficult to survey and full of con-tradictions: unlimited offerings of goods parallel with a new conscious-ness of environmental dangers and limited energy resources.

Art handicrafts have become more vital and have retaken much of the position they had during the 1950s and before their decline at the end of the 1960s. The craftsmen have formed new collective organiza-tions to exhibit, to sell their products and to support one another.

This development may sometimes seem to be a protest and indicative of a suspicion towards conditions of industry. A state commission re-port has stated that designers are being clearly under-utilized in in-dustry. An experimental program of information about design has been started but this has yet not changed the situation. At the same time, Swedish industry has experienced a very great structural change —not least in the glass, china, furniture and textile industries, that is, those industries which have always employed many designers. Com-panies have disappeared or have been bought up by larger industrial concerns working for a new export market.

The industrial designers have had to adjust to this new working situation. Some of them have been given the possibility of influencing the entire product development—from the idea for a product to the marketing—by being a part of a large working team, a more anony-mous and far-sighted job than that of the star designers of the 1950s and 1960s. Other designers have succeeded in finding new areas in which to work. Using appropriations for research and development, they have been able to carry out interesting projects—projects for the handicapped and the aged, improvements in the working environment, attempts to adjust products to technology using less energy.

The end of the 1970s is characterized by vitally flourishing art handicrafts, a struggling art industry aiming for new markets with its one-of-a-kind production, a new generation of designers with knowledge about the environment and natural resources who are tackling the long-run design problems of industry, breaking into new areas, and into the field of education for design which is still in its swaddling clothes.

Stockholm, July 1977 *Lennart Lindkvist*

Authors

Lennart Lindkvist (b. 1930), editor-in-chief of *FORM* magazine, 1963 —73. Since 1973, managing director of the Swedish Society of Industrial Design.

Gunilla Lundahl, B.A. (b. 1936), journalist and teacher at the Art Teachers' Training College, Stockholm. Editor of *Architect* magazine, 1971—77. Previously on the staff of *FORM* magazine, she has now begun working there again as of 1977.

Katja Waldén, B.A. (b. 1926), translator and freelance journalist, specializing in art and handicraft, writes for *FORM* and for the Stockholm newspaper *Expressen*. She has also helped prepare exhibitions at the Stockholm Museum of Modern Art and at the House of Culture in Stockholm.

Dag Widman, Ph.L. (b. 1924). Since 1966, chief curator of the Department of Applied Art at the Swedish National Museum of Fine Arts in Stockholm. In 1963—65 he was managing director at the Swedish Society of Industrial Design, and president in 1971—75.

Kerstin Wickman, B.A. (b. 1941). Since 1968, editorial staff member of *FORM* magazine, and co-editor since 1973. Instructor in environmental studies at the Art Teachers' Training College.

Dag Widman
The Swedish Art Industry 1917-1975

The Home Exhibition of 1917

If one wanted to give a precise date for the birth of the modern Swedish art industry, it would have to be 1917. At that time, a group of artists, representatives of a new generation, was engaged by a number of industries for the purpose of renewing production. With socially motivated goals, formulated by the Swedish Society of Industrial Design (Svenska Slöjdföreningen), an institution founded as early as 1845 and destined to play a central role in the coming developments, with young, enthusiastic artists whose eyes had been opened to a new and extensive field of work and with companies interested in unconventional production, conditions suddenly existed for a renewal of the Swedish art industry.

The immediate cause of this activity was an important exhibition arranged that year by the Society at the Liljevalch's Gallery in Stockholm. It was called the Home Exhibition and contained no fewer than 23 constructed and fully-furnished interiors created by young architects, as well as special sections for, among other things, glass and china. The idea was to show the working and lower middle classes new furniture and household articles which were of good esthetic and industrial quality, but inexpensive. Thus the objectives of the Swedish art industry in the coming decades were established. Gregor Paulsson, the main theoretician of this work and for a long period head of the Swedish Society of Industrial Design, wrote that it was a matter of "achieving a definitive change from the isolated production of individuals to the conscious work of a whole generation for a culture of form on a broad social basis."

Gunnar Asplund's much-admired chimney-corner room from the Home Exhibition of 1917, with sturdy spruce furniture, hooked rugs, blue and white wallpaper, light-colored curtains against darker woodwork and Wilhelm Kåge's "working-man's china" in the cabinet.

International success

But developments in the immediately following years were different from those forecast by the 1917 exhibition. The art industry of the 1920s was dominated by engraved, large, one-of-a-kind pieces of glass, unique ceramics and splendid intarsia furniture. Simon Gate and Edward Hald, the first artists at Orrefors, produced in the 1920s, in cooperation with skilful glassblowers and engravers, beautiful pieces in colored glass, so-called Graal glass, and engraved glass. It was primarily Orrefors glass that led the way for the international success of the new Swedish art industry. The first big victory was at the Paris Exposition of 1925, but as early as 1921 *The Studio* had contained a richly illustrated article about Orrefors' art glass. The graceful Swedish pavilion at the Paris Exposition also contained delightful furniture by Carl Malmsten, china by the country's foremost ceramic artist, Wilhelm Kåge from Gustavsberg, and silver. Two years later the Swedish art industry had an exhibition at the Metropolitan Museum in New York, the first time a European country had been invited to arrange an exhibition of this type.

Functionalism and social involvement

Thus the Swedish art industry was on the way to international fame, with the emphasis on the more exclusive type of production. But toward the end of the 1920s, new influences were reaching Sweden. These came from the *Bauhaus* movement and the new, socially involved architecture which in Sweden was soon to be given the name "functionalism."

The Society of Industrial Design took the initiative for a large exhibition in Stockholm in 1930, an exhibition which became the foremost manifestation of the functionalistic *avant-garde*. The men primarily responsible for the exhibition were the Society's Gregor Paulsson, the leader of the new movement in Sweden, and the architect Gunnar Asplund. The exhibition aroused a storm of debate of unprecedented proportions. It laid the foundation for new thinking about housing, built on a broad, social basis, and showed unconventional furnishing, emphasizing function, material, method of production and standardization as the norms of design. Changes also took place in the art industry. For instance, engraved thin glass was abandoned in favor of allowing heavy masses of crystal to speak for themselves. The china industry introduced stackable, easily-washed tableware.

The international success of the Swedish art industry continued during the 1930s, culminating in the Paris Exposition of 1937 and the World Fair in New York in 1939. In time, the strict functionalism was modified, and the demand for serviceability was combined with a softer design and the beginnings of a movement toward color and patterns. In the field of furniture, Bruno Mathsson, an original and talented designer, introduced his bentwood furniture. The Orrefors glass company got a new artist, Vicke Lindstrand.

Art handicraft flourishes

The isolation of the Second World War meant, among other things, a shortage of materials and manpower, which hindered the spread of mass-produced goods. But individual handicrafts flourished all the more. A new generation of artists was engaged by industry. A typical representative was Stig Lindberg, who, at Gustavsberg, divided his time between unique stoneware, flowered faience and formal tableware. Barbro Nilsson became the artistic leader of the Märta Måås-Fjetterström AB and, with her colleagues, Marianne Richter and Ann-Mari Forsberg, played a leading role in the textile art of the 1940s and 1950s. Cool, Nordic flowers blossomed in the printed cloths and faiences of the Jobs family up in the province of Dalarna.

At this time, the Society of Industrial Design initiated a systematic study of household articles in order to acquire a more precise knowledge as a basis for the work of the designer. This was intensified in the succeeding decades and led, in the 1960s, to the establishment of a separate Furniture Research Institute.

Good everyday wares

During the war and the 1950s considerable changes took place in Swedish society. The tremendous migration from the countryside into the cities, large new groups of citizens with higher standards of living in new surroundings, increasing international exchanges, the intensification of construction work, particularly in the public sector—all these meant good times for the art industry in the 1950s. This led to the great breakthrough for designers in production; companies making furniture, textiles, glass and china vied in employing designers.

One can see in this period a surprisingly high average standard in everyday goods with the demands for beautiful form and proper usability satisfied. And the chain stores saw to it that these wares were available all over the country. There was a number of exhibitions both inside and outside Sweden. The biggest event of the decade was the H 55 exhibition in Helsingborg, which had no less than 1,100,000 visitors during a few sunny summer months in 1955. Again the initiative was taken by the Society of Industrial Design, with its director,

Åke H. Huldt, as manager. The exhibition showed the rather impressive results of the work of a few decades in furnishing and housing.

From 1954 to 1957, a large exhibition called Design in Scandinavia toured the United States and Canada. It was the result of the growing collaboration of the four Nordic countries (Denmark, Finland, Norway, Sweden) in the field of utility art. These four countries also aroused a great deal of attention at the Triennale in Milan.

A new consciousness

The 1960s were the decade of violent change. People began to question quality as a stable value. "Buy-use-throw-away" was a phrase in the debate which, among other things, questioned the value of the craftsmanlike finish and lasting quality of the art industry. Many people saw pop art as a liberation from the formality of designed products. At the same time, art crafts were developing toward more and more marked individualism. Toward the end of the 1960s, people began to notice the reverse side of the welfare state in the form of the littering and pollution of the environment. Solidarity with the developing countries began to increase. The new political consciousness put the common environment before the individual product, an attitude which struck mostly at exclusive art handicrafts.

The first part of the 1970s will be remembered for an increased appreciation of handicrafts as a meaningful form of production, supported by a growing sector of the population. The young artists, on the other hand, are less interested in devoting themselves to the art industry, which is in a noticeable period of transition involving far-reaching rationalization of production and the merging of smaller units into larger ones. The designer, working in industry or on a consultant basis, has a clearer profile than previously. In collaboration with other experts, he gives form to parts of the environment, such as, for example, a complete hygiene system or he attempts to solve the problems of the handicapped.

Common for both the artists who work on a handicrafts basis and the designers of industry is a new consciousness of man's difficult and hazardous situation in the world.

Katja Waldén Glass

Ownership relations

The Swedish glass companies are small by international standards, and their main production is decorative glass, although there is also production of household glass and lighting fixtures. Their total sales (1975) amounted to just over Skr 200 million, of which Skr 85 million was for exports. At the same time Sweden imported glass —primarily cheap household glass—for about Skr 70 million.

During the 1960s, the competitive position of the glass companies drastically changed. Making glass by hand is expensive, and the wages of Swedish glass workers are relatively high. There has been a tremendous increase in the importation of cheap glass. Some companies have been forced out of business, and those that are left must try to rationalize their methods and to combine into groups in order to keep up with the competition.

In the middle of the 1960s, Kosta—the oldest Swedish glass company, founded in the middle of the 1700s and well known for its fine crystal, its skilful engravers and polishers—combined with Åfors (which had everyday table glass as a speciality and the versatile Bertil Vallien as its designer) and Boda (which had achieved a special profile with eager experimentation, primarily under Erik Höglund).

During the 1970s, the companies continued their efficiency measures, and particularly their fusions. Åfors cut down its stock from 8,000 to 1,500 products. The most noticed fusion was the one that took place in 1975, when the Kosta-Boda group, which is responsible for 20 per cent of the glass production in Sweden, merged in a large industry which includes, among others, the Finnish porcelain factory, Arabia, the Finnish Notsjö glass works and the Norwegian Egersund faience factory, as well as the Swedish Rörstrand porcelain factory. Orrefors

Glass workers at Orrefors' glassworks: cutting on a foot.

had, already in 1971, ceased being a family business and became part of a large industry; furthermore, Strömbergshyttan was bought out by Orrefors a few years ago. These ownership relations have their interest, since they also affect production and design. The glass produced by the Kosta-Boda group now is a part of stocks covering objects for the whole table, in glass and porcelain. With a common drive, on a larger scale than any individual works could afford, the emphasis has now been focussed abroad, with hopes for increased exports.

Furthermore, the glass companies tried to overcome the crisis by seeking new markets, experimenting with new forms and reducing the

Gunnar Cyrén:
bowl and goblets
in Graal technique
with patterns in
opalescent white.
Orrefors, 1977.

Olle Alberius:
blown salad bowl.
Orrefors, 1973.

number of items kept in stock. The social responsibility of the companies is also a heavy burden; they have skilful blowers, engravers and polishers who must have employment.

A further difficulty is that the debate on improved working environment, which has been carried on rather intensively in Sweden in the 1970s, strikes the glass works particularly hard. However fascinating this crafts industry may be, it must be condemned from almost every environmental point of view. Blowing glass is risky, and the heat and the noise exceed all approved values.

Most Swedish glass is produced in a limited area in the southern province of Småland, within a radius of about nine kilometers from Växjö. Within this circle lie about thirty manual-production glass companies, which are active today. Together they employ about 2,700 workers. The largest is the Kosta-Boda group—Kosta, Boda, Åfors, and Johansfors glass works—with 750 employees, followed by Orrefors, which includes the Orrefors, Sandvik, Alsterfors and Flygsfors works and which has a total of 500 employees. After them comes the Krona group, a sales organization for four glass works, with 300 employees, which was formed in the early 1970s and was dissolved during the summer of 1977. The other glass works employ between 20 and 200 people each.

The glass works

In the beginning of October 1966, Orrefors inaugurated a new factory. At that time, most of the artists responsible for the greatness and global reputation of Orrefors were still working there: Gunnar Cyrén, Ingeborg Lundin, Sven Palmqvist, Nils Landberg and John Selbing. *Ingeborg Lundin* created ethereal one-of-a-kind pieces and large, shimmering, graceful glass bubbles, with abstract decoration in engraving or relief. Young *Gunnar Cyrén* broke radically with Orrefors' traditions by making "pop" glass with stained layers of white, red, blue and green, generous goblets in opalized white with striped feet in fresh color combinations, rustically decorated glass and engraved bowls and bottles.

Ten years later, the picture had partically changed. In Orrefors' fine glass museum, one has a splendid opportunity of surveying the company's influence on Swedish glass. It still manufactures some of the sets

*Lars Hellsten: glass decoration in the entrance hall of the Värnamo Hospital.
Orrefors, 1975.*

and forms of glass which have become classical and which have contributed to the worldwide reputation of Orrefors. But the range has been narrowed and adjusted to the market. The company has a section for experimental and one-of-a-kind goods and a section for exclusive base products and more fashion-based products.

Olle Alberius (formerly at Rörstrand), Lars Hellsten (until 1972 with Skruf) and Eva Englund (formerly at Pukeberg) are the designers behind Orrefors' new line. Among the permanently employed designers are also *Carl Fagerlund,* who is responsible for lamps and lamp fittings, and the latest employee Wiktor Berndt. Gunnar Cyrén, Jan Johansson, Owe Elvén and the Danish designer, Henning Koppel, work as freelancers.

Olle Alberius is continuing and renewing the great Orrefors line from the 1920s, with his vases and bowls in crystal, with cut, etched or colored decoration. *Eva Englund* worked with free glass sculptures: hands, grapes, flowers, and was especially fascinated by the properties of glass as a flowing mass. She designed "spun glass," in which the strips of glass meet and cross in bowl-like forms—but without fulfilling the function of a bowl. This was one way of exploiting the character of glass as a liquid—a game, but a game with interesting consequences. At Orrefors she has been successful in her use of the Graal technique which Edward Hald and Simon Gate made world famous in the 1920s.

Lars Hellsten exhibited his free glass sculptures, fantastic towers and gazebos and bubbling vase forms, at the show called Glasharmonika in 1965. He was greeted with delight as a welcome and humorous renewer in the art of Swedish glass. Together with Erik Höglund and Bertil Vallien, he was included in the epithet, "Swedish Neo-Baroque" in glass. Lars Hellsten was also a sculptor and ceramist to start with, and he likes to blow his glass in forms which he whittles out himself. He contrasts round, puffy forms with straight, geometric ones. He captures the light in the rotund surfaces of the thick crystal, and one's eye is constantly being led on through the new, unexpected play of lines in his creations, which are often generously large.

At Kosta the virtuoso *Vicke Lindstrand* in the 1960s created glass with polyoptic reflection effects and glass sculptures, while *Mona*

Eva Englund: bowl in Graal technique with dark-blue bottom. Orrefors, 1975.

Signe Persson-Melin: flame-proof teapot with heating base and teacup. Boda Nova, 1971.

Morales-Schildt added something new to decorative glass with multi-colored, polished glass cubes. Today, the designers at Kosta-Boda, are Ann Wärff, Paul Hoff, Bertil Vallien, Ulrica Hydman-Vallien, Signe Persson-Melin, Monica Backström, Rolf Sinnemark and, since 1976, Claes-Göran Tinbäck. Among the designers who work as free-lancers for Kosta-Boda are Lisa Bauer, Sigurd Persson, Erik Höglund and Göran Wärff.

Erik Höglund started as a sculptor and his feeling for the three-dimensional is also obvious in his glass works. In addition to glass, he devoted himself at Boda to ironsmithing, furniture and polychrome wood reliefs. He also utilized his skill as a smith when he designed candelabras with glass dangles. His seals, medals and early bubbly, colored glass in orange and turquoise and his brandy flasks with their expansive, rustic forms have a careless charm but express, above all, an almost baroque feeling for life. Some of his "offside glass," ordinary glass forms which seem to have failed and to have crumpled, may seem to be an imprecise, but effective, form of protest. Since 1974 he has worked as a free-lancer in the Kosta-Boda group.

An extravagant feeling for life also characterizes *Monica Backström,* who has, joyfully and without prejudice, tried out the many possibilities of glass, particularly in combination with metal. During the 1970s, she has developed playful glass sculptures in the form of eggs and mushrooms, with colored or etched decoration. *Rolf Sinnemark* has also devoted himself to glass sculpture with, among other things, naturalistic "eggs" and glass bells, which he calls "solaris." But primarily he designs table glass for Boda.

Toward the end of the 1960s, Boda Nova introduced a series which includes fireproof glass in combination with cork in tiles and handles, stoneware bowls and wooden cutting boards. *Signe Persson-Melin* has been responsible for the glass and ceramics part of this program. She is a ceramist, but made her debut as a glass designer with "Glass by the Square" (Glas i fyrkant): generous simple cans and bottles, blown in wooden forms. Her collection for Boda Nova includes flameproof soufflé and gratin bowls, pots and deep frying pans, tea and coffee pots and warming tiles. All these objects are well thought out, well balanced and have the same natural charm contained by everything designed by Signe Persson-Melin. The series has been supplemented with "Boda Blom," in which she varies the same basic form, with a broad base, for three wide-mouthed and three narrow vases in clear glass. These are typical of Signe Persson-Melin's way of working; she starts from a need, creates prototypes for the everyday articles and tries them out herself: "I make the things I think I need myself. There aren't very many of them, but I can defend them. After all, I'm not unique."

Bertil Vallien, who was originally a sculptor and a ceramist, came to Åfors as a designer in 1963 and was one of those who created the "new" Swedish glass. He expresses himself very freely in glass but also designs robust table glass. He mixes techniques and colors, often in the same piece of glass. His round, pouchy bottles seem to be swelling under their own power, and glass forms are attached to one another in such a natural and spontaneous way that they seem to grow organically and yet retain their strictness of design. He has more and more devoted himself to free glass sculpture and is now building whole "landscapes" in glass in which he utilizes the various effects of the material.

Bertil Vallien expresses something like a statement of aims, as follows: "I think that traditional handicrafts must be changed greatly to get away from the cult of *things.* They must be more actively stimulating to the imagination and approach the free arts." And he summarizes his views of the designers' job at the glass company: "Free experimentation is often called, by the managers, 'playing around,' but that is decidedly the wrong expression. Freedom to experiment with forms and materials is absolutely necessary and extremely serious. It is our form of research."

"I want to express something playful, to show another world beyond the usual. I want to paint figures on glass, so they can fly and run, try new wings on new winds, until the bubble bursts." *Ulrica Hydman-Vallien* at Åfors looks upon the creation of glass unconventionally. For her, glass is just one of the materials she expresses herself in; she is also a ceramist and a painter. Her playfulness and imaginativeness seem endless when she paints butterflies, flowers, animals and human figures on charmingly carelessly blown glass. But her primitivism has a double

Bertil Vallien: sand-blasted vase with iridescent surface. Kosta-Boda, 1976.

Bertil Vallien: "Strong Powers," hot-blasted black bowl. Kosta-Boda, 1976.

Ann Wärff: glass sculpture in opalescent white. Kosta-Boda, 1975.

foundation. It is not just naive and innocent—it is also enchanting, magic.

Ann and *Göran Wärff,* who won the Lunning Prize in 1968, have invented their own technique. They allow the molten glass to run down into a form with a hollowed-out space and to cool. The result is remarkably vital glass bowls, with heavy drops hanging from the edges. They also make glass plates with flowing colors in violent whirls, large plastic-like platters and massive glass sculptures with bright colors—all marked by their view of glass as a living, organic mass, possible to form, to stop and to master—but only to a certain point: "We seldom start with an idea. We listen, watch the molten glass, the light, the glitter.

Paul Hoff: "Two Jaguars," plate in single and double underlay. Kosta-Boda, 1975.

Why does it look like that? Why does it act like that? It keeps us excited. You can violate glass, but that is hardly interesting . . . And we work with clearly functional everyday things, too. We must do both. One leads to the other. It is important to us that we are part of a social situation, as at Kosta glass works."

During the 1970s Ann Wärff has given her material more and more freedom, inspired by the free glass creation in, among other places, the United States and Sweden. These "organic landscapes" sometimes turn into tremendous and fantastic glass formations, making use of all her technical skill and all the techniques she has mastered—etching, sand blasting, soldering. In 1974 Göran Wärff emigrated to Australia, but he

Lisa Bauer: "Wild Strawberries," crystal bowl with engraving; form by Sigurd Persson. Kosta-Boda, beginning of the 1970s.

still works for the Kosta group as a free-lancer.

Also in 1974, the young designer *Paul Hoff* came to Kosta, where he has made himself known with, among other things, bowls and vases with pictures of animals, not naturalistic but slightly stylized, languishing and sophisticated, but with a character of their own.

Sigurd Persson, a many-sided designer, has designed glass on a free-lance basis for Kosta: simple glass forms in red, orange, yellow, blue, with sparse decoration in the form of signs. An interesting case of cooperation was started when Sigurd Persson joined up with graphic artist *Lisa Bauer*, who draws beautifully naturalistic patterns with flowers and plants which are then etched into glass forms by Sigurd Persson.

The Skruf, Gullaskruf, Åseda and Målerås works together formed the Krona group Co., with a common sales organization. Gullaskruf's specialty has traditionally been pressed glass, and in that technique *Kjell Blomberg* has created "Tiara," a series of bowls. Among the works' other designers are Bo Borgström, Bengt Edenfalk, Lisa and Gunnar Larson and Marianne Westman (the last three also active as ceramists), who have designed both decorative and household glass.

At the Lindshammar company, which has specialized in architectural glass, among other things, *Christer Sjögren* and *Tom Möller* have introduced hand-made modules of uncolored glass which have great possibilities for variation. Christer Sjögren, previously a sculptor in wood, has, since 1963, been designing vases and table glassware with sculptural forms and a sober, decorative effect. Gunnar Ander, Catharina Åselius-Lidbeck and Marguerite Walfridsson have designed decorative glass for this company.

There also exists artistic glass outside the glass works. A few young designers have built their own works.

Åsa Brandt in Torshälla makes her own glass from start to finish—a unique situation in Sweden. She says of her work and her technique: "Here in my workshop I want to create glass which is a product of my personal imagination, and in which the detailed work can be permitted to take a long time. I also have the possibility of changing the original idea in the course of working on it, of letting the glass help me. Naturally, I have no interest in manufacturing purely utilitarian products— that's for the glass companies. I want to use glass as a living material that is undeniably fascinating both to work with and to look at. Of course, I put my ideas on paper before I start to make my glass, but my drawings are just sketches of ideas, and the final form grows out of the work itself." Among Åsa Brandt's works are glass sculptures in soft forms, inviting us to touch them and caress them. She wants us literally to *feel* the material. *Ulla Forsell* and *Eva Ullberg* also blow their own glass.

Another result of the rather troublesome situation in glass is that young Swedish designers are going abroad. For example, *Ove* and *Bir-*

Ulla Forsell: "Glass Garden," sculpture in mixed technique. Her own workshop, 1977.

gitta Thorsén are designing glass for the Venini glass works in Murano.

The liberation, the vital experimenting and the crossing of boundaries which characterized the 1960s in Swedish glass and led many people to speak of "Swedish Neo-Baroque" were followed by a period of belt-tightening as business fell off toward the end of the decade.

Through various types of efficiency measures, as we have said, an attempt is being made to make the future of the Swedish glass works secure. A certain stabilizing effect has been achieved, but the balance is delicate. The margins are narrow, and there are strict limits to experimentation. The trump card is the skill of the designers and their love of their material. Swedish glass is emphasizing quality and exclusiveness and leaving the market for household glass open for foreign imports.

Dag Widman Ceramics

In 1960, *Wilhelm Kåge* died. As an artist at Gustavsberg since 1917, he had played a more important role in his field and had had a greater influence on his successors than any other Swedish ceramist before him. During the 1930s, he created a number of designs for tableware service under the influence of the functionalistic ideas which incarnated the principles of good, sturdy everyday goods. At the same time, he designed a new type of stoneware, the so-called "Farsta-goods," in which, despite influences from China and Mexico, his powerful, independent creativity achieved full expression. "For Wilhelm Kåge, ceramics was a universe, and life existed in order for him to discover and artistically express its dizzying possibilities," wrote the design specialist Arthur Hald on his death.

About 1960, the situation in ceramics began to change palpably in Sweden. In 1947, Wilhelm Kåge had hired a young artist at Gustavsberg called *Anders Liljefors*. In 1956, Liljefors exhibited in Stockholm a group of ceramic objects which may be described as an important point in the development of modern Swedish ceramics toward informal freedom. He literally broke down the harmonic forms which had for so long dominated Swedish ceramics, inspired by classical Chinese ceramics. With a new technique, sand moulding, he had an instrument to play on which gave him new and hitherto unseen forms. Not least in monumental works in connection with architecture, this new method had great significance. During the 1960s, Anders Liljefors developed an intensive, at times furious, creation of ceramics which became one of the most personal contributions in Swedish ceramics. He died in 1970.

In general the last few years of the 1950s involved obvious changes in Swedish art handicrafts, the most striking feature of which was the crossing of boundaries in the direction of free art. *Hertha Hillfon* made a significant debut in 1959. The year before, she had shown her ceramics for the first time in public. Her first works, large painted platters, vessels in the shape of figures and free sculptures, immediately aroused interest. With small strings of clay, she rolled and baked a world of forms appealing to the imagination. She worked rapidly, under the influence of an experience or a mood; it might be a meeting with someone, the soft, rolling cooing of doves or music—Bach, Bartók or jazz. In the middle of the 1960s, a new, realistic simplicity began to mark her works. Everyday objects, gloves, shoes, furniture, were transformed from the world of chance occurrence into the eternity of stoneware. Today she is one of our most important sculptors. She is imaginative, surprising, a master of technique. In the past few years, her works have been marked by great simplicity and purity. The freedom Hertha Hillfon achieved in her ceramic creations has been of great significance for practically all the ceramists who came after her. She has created larger works for, among others, the Operakällaren restaurant and the Hotel Anglais in Stockholm and a monument, "In Honor of the Walloons," at the Lövsta Iron Works, about 100 kilometers north of Stockholm.

Parallel with a similar development both on the continent of Europe and in the United States, after the emergence of Hertha Hillfon many Swedish ceramists have primarily devoted themselves to non-utilitarian ceramics. Up to now, the most important of these has been *Britt-Ingrid Persson*, "BIP," who made her debut with an exhibition in 1966. At that time, the art critic, Eugen Wretholm, wrote: "When I see her ragged, broken egg forms, I get the feeling of complete self-exposure. The small, white abstract figures have heads like quivering flower chalices. Put together in groups, they form fields of psychic power like Giacometti's bronze plates. Her forms are not like anything else I have ever seen. The works of this debutant have a tone of pain-filled beauty which makes it exciting to wait for her subsequent development" (*FORM,* no 5, 1966). Since then, Britt-Ingrid Persson has with greater and greater intensity involved herself in man's situation in the society of today. With irony and humor (and also with distaste), she asks questions in her works, sometimes too obviously, often with manifold meanings. Her main subject is man's difficulty in achieving meaningful self-devel-

Hertha Hillfon: sculpture in unglazed stoneware, 1975.

Hertha Hillfon: "The Box," unglazed stoneware, 1969.

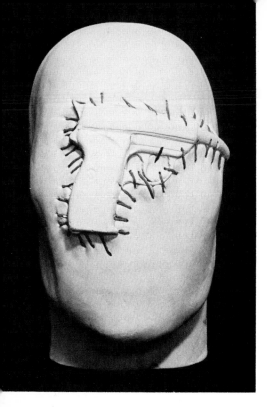

*Britt-Ingrid Persson,
"BIP:" "Environment-
al Inheritance," stone-
ware sculpture, 1974.*

*Britt-Ingrid Persson:
"Embryo for a New
Earth" and "Woman—
Human Being," sculp-
ture group in stoneware,
1974.*

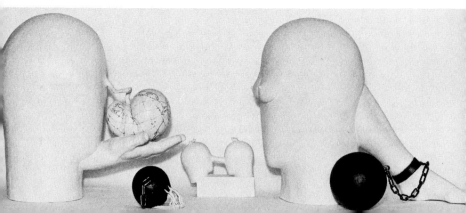

opment in a crass, materialistic society, man's lack of contact with organic nature, both inside and outside of himself. She has the broadest ceramic knowledge but prefers to work without glazes in dry, porcelain-like stoneware. No effects are allowed to get in the way of the questions she asks. She prefers the miniature format, but she has also done larger wall compositions. She does not consider herself primarily a ceramist, but she thinks that in clay she has found a material which follows her intentions well.

In her consistency and her biting criticism of society, Britt-Ingrid Persson is *sui generis* in Swedish ceramics. But there are those who sometimes work in the same field. *Gösta Grähs* has given a realistic and expressive form to his experience of environmental pollution and the spread of poisons, particularly in his depictions of insects and other animals. He often works with a combination of red chamotte refractory goods and porcelain clay. He has a workshop together with *Kerstin Hörnlund,* who has done lyrical reliefs and masks. Together, they also manufacture robust everyday stoneware.

Bertil Vallien and his wife, *Ulrica Hydman-Vallien,* were also among the remarkable representatives of ceramic freedom in the 1960s. For a few years at the beginning of the decade, Bertil Vallien was active as ceramist on the American west coast and not without success. Since his return to Sweden, he has primarily become famous for his glass. But he has continued to work in clay, with new, dynamically designed ceramic pieces which he sometimes paints in bright plastic colors. To admirers of classic stoneware influenced by the Chinese Sung ceramics—those lovers of glaze nuances—Vallien's gaudily painted ceramics seemed like a blow in the stomach. Ulrica Hydman-Vallien, instead, appeared as a somewhat primitive artist with traditions in the ceramics of folk art. Her storybook castles and figures have both joy and humor.

Ulla Viotti began her career as a ceramist with rather conventional glazed stoneware. But during the latter part of the 1960s she began to use a new way of working. She has done large works with combinations of stoneware and tarred ropes. One of her works is called "Mountain-side;" it works with both visual and acoustical effects, combined with the tarry smell of the rope.

Ulla Viotti: stoneware relief in white clay, 50 by 90 cm., 1976.

Ulrica Hydman-Vallien: stoneware sculpture, 1976.

Nils Gunnar Zander in his workshop working on stoneware sculptures: totem poles and masks.

Lillemor Petersson, active in Göteborg, works, like Britt-Ingrid Persson, with matters of current social interest, but without the latter's ambiguity. "Monument to a Bureaucrat's Birth" is the name of one of her works in which she uses small reliefs, in the style of a comic strip, to describe the changes in a man.

However, most of the free ceramists do not involve themselves in social debate but let their works reflect general moods and conditions.

Märit Lindberg-Freund has worked preferably with completely white, glazed or unglazed forms. She began with simple bowls and vases, but she has later devoted herself more and more to free sculpture. In simple, soft forms, she has given expression for healthy, pure

Henrik Allert: head of a horse, stoneware sculpture, 1976.

sensualism or in reliefs in blue and white depicted the meeting of sea and shore. *Nils Gunnar Zander* made his debut in 1971. He treats the clay quite unconventionally, running it through a meat grinder, pressing cloth against it to get the desired surface. His forms were formerly largely vegetative; more recently he has made, among other things, expressive human masks, totem poles and sculptures of sheep. *Henrik Allert* also is among those who made a debut in the 1970s. With his expressive sculptures of seagulls and other animals, he is a sensitive and original ceramic sculptor. *Dagmar Norell* has given expression for quietness and serenity in torso-like vessel forms. *Päivi Ernkvist,* who comes from Finland, works less with presenting objects and more with overreaching ideas. Under the theme, "To the workers," she achieved ensemble play among figures and objects, marked by quietness and reflection.

The ceramists named up to now are representatives of a dominant movement in Swedish ceramics during the past few years. Their works are largely sculptural and are marked by involvement, freedom and individuality.

During the 20th century the main emphasis in ceramic creation has been more and more moved from the factories to individual workshops. *Ingrid* and *Erich Triller* started a workshop in the little village of Tobo, 120 kilometers north of Stockholm, as early as the 1930s. With classical techniques of throwing and a splendid register of glazes, they managed a highly consistent and important production until their activity was broken off when Erich Triller died in 1972.

Eva Lagerheim: "Dog,"
stoneware, 1975.

One of the most sensitive and skilful ceramists during the same period was *Grete Möller,* active in Stockholm. The province of Skåne, in southernmost Sweden, has long had a rich ceramic tradition. There *Signe Persson-Melin* appeared in the 1950s with her rustic useful objects, full of character. Nowadays she works primarily with glass. A number of good ceramists work around the town of Höganäs in Skåne, including the original *Åke Holm* and *Rolf Palm,* who make powerfully formed stoneware. *Gustav Kraitz* has made stoneware in a large format associated with the environment and is experimenting with glazes based on the Chinese tradition.

The large factories

In the 20th century, the large porcelain factories, primarily Rörstrand (founded in 1726) and Gustavsberg (founded in 1827), have been the most important centers of Swedish ceramics. Both of these factories have employed a group of full-time artists. The artists have had the possibility of working both with tableware in mass production and with one-of-a-kind or few-of-a-kind objects. This way of working has been, without a doubt, advantageous for their creativity.

The leading artist at Rörstrand up until the beginning of the 1970s was *Carl-Harry Stålhane.* He was very productive and devoted himself to powerful and dramatic stoneware formed into vases, bowls and sculptures, porcelain tableware for homes and restaurants and wall decorations for public buildings. In 1964, for example, he made a relief in stoneware for a bank in Kansas City, a tremendous ceramic landscape which is one of the largest ceramic works ever made in Sweden. In his restaurant tableware, he methodically studied stackability, suitability for washing in machine and for run-off when drying.

In 1973 Stålhane left Rörstrand, which he had served for 34 years, and started a ceramic workshop of his own just north of the city of Lidköping. With greater intensity than ever before, he continued there his mighty production of stoneware, which also includes quiet and sensitively made works related to the Chinese glazing tradition.

Hertha Bengtson specialized even more in tableware and has achieved considerable success with pure and simple forms, with simple decora-

Stig Lindberg: "The Beach," stoneware decoration for a swimming hall, school of the Swedish Confederation of Trade Unions. Gustavsberg, 1976.

Bertil Lundgren: tableware of feldspar porcelain. Rörstrand, 1977.

Karin Björquist: stackable tableware in bone china. Gustavsberg, 1970-71.

tion. In the beginning of the 1950s, for example, she created the "Koka" tableware, which today may be considered a classic. In 1969 she left Rörstrand and now is working successfully with the German factories, Rosenthal and Thomas. *Marianne Westman* in the 1960s renewed decorated everyday porcelain with robust, healthy decorations inspired by folk art. She also has left Rörstrand. *Sylvia Leuchovius* has devoted herself to decorated wall plaques and tableware decorations.

Since 1964 the Rörstrand factory has been part of the Upsala-Ekeby company. In 1975 the Finnish porcelain factory, Arabia, was also merged with the company. The newly formed Arabia-Rörstrand company now also includes the Norwegian faience factory, Egersund. It was in connection with these fusions that the old staff of designers left Rörstrand. At present, the company has only three designers employed: Sylvia Leuchovius, Bertil Lundgren and Jacqueline Lynn.

Gustavsberg has a strong, individualistic group of artists working at the factory. The leading artist, after Wilhelm Kåge, has been *Stig Lindberg,* who came to Gustavsberg as early as 1937. A renewer of ceramic sculpture and painted faience during the 1940s, he has, with his seemingly inexhaustible imagination, been able to realize his ideas in the most disparate areas. His desire to revolt against formal conventions has always marked his work with stoneware and, at the beginning, his work with tableware too. During the 1950s and 1960s, however, he was the creator of some of the best tableware ever made in Sweden. Of late, his stoneware has become more classic in form. Through his production and his position as chief teacher of ceramics at the State School of Arts and Design in Stockholm 1957—70, he has exercised a considerable influence on contemporary Swedish ceramics.

Berndt Friberg came to Gustavsberg as early as the middle of the 1930s. He became a master potter and Kåge's leading assistant. Since the middle of the 1940s, he has emerged more and more as an independent artist. With controlled forms in exquisite proportions, inspired by the classical Chinese stoneware, he has documented his mastery over the years. His primary means of expression is glazes. Originally understated and delicate, these have with the years become clearer and more intensive. He says that he can achieve two hundred variants in glaze.

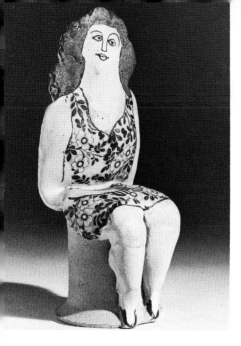

Lisa Larson: figure in stoneware. Gustavsberg, 1975.

Margareta Hennix: stoneware pots. Gustavsberg, 1977.

Consistently, he has followed his own way through the changing winds of popular taste. Friberg retired in the 1970s, and since then has been working part-time.

Karin Björquist came to Gustavsberg in 1950 as a representative of the new generation of artists. Highly personal in her work, she also has marked preference for anonymity. In the middle of the 1950s, she designed a well thought-out set of tableware called "Vardag" (Everyday). Her work always has a dispassionate clarity of form. It is strict and decisive, but it does not preclude gentleness.

Since the 1960s she has worked mostly with monumental jobs. In 1963 along with architect Kjell Abramson, she designed one of Stockholm's underground railway stations, the one in Maria Square, which, with its profiled walls in warm colors, has held up remarkably well. She made monumental tile stoves for the Swedish embassies in Moscow and Paris. With liberating purity and simplicity in form she has shown the tremendous possibility of the ceramic material for use in public buildings. She is also responsible for splendid tableware in bone china and ceramics ("Brown Line," 1972) and for vessels for holding flowers.

Lisa Larson has made her greatest contribution quantitatively with mass-produced decorative items: unpretentious, lively small sculptures of people and animals which have become very popular. She has also made one-of-a-kind stoneware pieces with a personal touch in the design. The artists' circle at Gustavsberg also includes *Britt-Louise Sundell,* who has composed tableware and originally decorated objects in white stoneware, and *Bengt Berglund.* In highly individual, sometimes bizarre sculptures, often created from rolled clay, the latter has given expression to growth and the unexpected. In conscious protest against beautiful glazes, he works with dry, light clay surfaces, articulated on the surface.

The youngest of the artists working at Gustavsberg is *Margareta Hennix,* who has designed both splendid useful objects and free works in a neo-romantic style, and *Paul Hoff,* who has largely devoted himself to mass-produced small sculptures of caricatures of birds. Since 1975, Paul Hoff has been employed by the Kosta-Boda glass works.

The new everyday ceramics of the 20th century

Despite stray examples of individually formed ceramics at the big factories, their standard production has been struck by rationalizing in form and decoration, which has created a need for varied everyday objects with a personal touch. Now, well into the 1970s, a number of ceramists have turned their attention to everyday objects which they either give a palpably individual character or, in a style of neo-primitivism, adjust to an earlier tradition. *Eva Sjögren* has long worked with useful objects in stoneware which she has developed to perfection in pure, simple, highly functional forms. Several of the younger ceramists work in the same spirit. *Gunilla Kropp* consciously associates with the tradition in her robust stoneware objects. *Charlotte Alexanderson* prefers to work with everyday objects in white porcelain clay formed to whole, even figures. *Birgitta Watz-Wåreus* produces ceramic pictures, clay with impressions of plants, but she has a basic production of simply made everyday useful objects. *Mari Almqvist* kneads and rolls the clay into imaginative bowls and platters. She often provides them with simple, primitive decoration in cobalt and glazes them at high temperatures.

In this way the small workshops have again taken over the everyday ceramics, varied in form and decoration, which used to be made by the large factories but which has disappeared from them in the inevitable technical development with its accompanying demands for profitability.

In 1975 an association of 23 ceramic artists and glass designers was formed with the name Blås & knåda (Blow & Throw). This association is presented in more detail on page 147.

Katja Waldén Silver

A certain stringent reserve long characterized Swedish silver. *Jacob Ängman,* active as teacher and artistic leader for Guldsmedsaktiebolaget returned to ideas from the great period in Swedish silver, the 18th century, when, in the 1920s and 1930s, he created his simple, noble silver pieces. *Wiwen Nilsson's* church silver, jewelry and decorative pieces have a geometric clarity which is inspired both by cubism and by medieval forms, while *Erik Fleming* at the Borgila Studio cultivated a reserved, classical style.

This style was passed on through *Sven Arne Gillgren*, chief teacher of metal work at the State School of Arts and Design (1955—70) and Jacob Ängman's successor. He in turn educated a new generation of young silversmiths. His experience as an industrial designer also enriched his silver work, which became simpler and clearer. During his time as teacher at the State School of Arts and Design, industrial design, too, received more emphasis in the curriculum.

The beginnings of the 1960s were dominated by two extraordinarily skilful silver artists: Sigurd Persson and Torun Bülow-Hübe. *Sigurd Persson,* with his amazing versatility, has covered practically every field in silver: tankards, vases, bowls, candelabra, jewelry. His fine feeling for, and virtuoso treatment of, the material is combined with the satisfaction of functional demands, and there the influence of Sigurd Persson, the industrial designer, can be traced. His gold and silver jewelry stimulates the imagination, with its free forms and often exquisite combinations with precious stones.

Torun Bülow-Hübe's jewelry, watches, bowls and tableware may be considered as free artistic compositions, sculptures in silver. In her jewelry she exhibits great boldness while retaining the decorative function. Torun Bülow-Hübe now lives in Germany and works for Georg Jensen in Denmark.

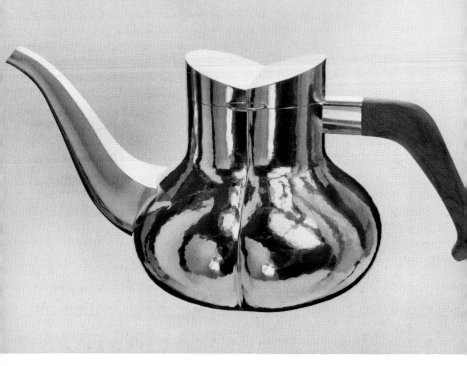

Sigurd Persson: teapot in silver with juniper handle, 1976.

In September 1965, when the National Museum of Fine Arts invited about fifty young Swedish silversmiths to exhibit their works, this was an interesting inventory of what modern Swedish silversmithing had to offer and, at the same time, a display of new tendencies and a new kind of freedom which were to develop richly during the following years— despite the 35 per cent sales tax, which logically should have hampered sales. Not since the 18th century, actually, had Swedish silver experienced such a flourishing period as during the beginning and middle of the 1960s, both quantitatively and qualitatively. The silversmiths reached a new and broader audience and also received numerous commissions for churches and other public places.

Birger Haglund introduced this new, promising freedom as early as his debut in 1964. He switched from geometric forms to a more romantic style, influenced by nature, and has since developed greater and greater freedom and skill, in earrings which seem to be cut out of thin silver plate, with large, vital forms combined to create a mobile, light-catching jewel. He uses unpolished Swedish stones and dares to mix such materials as plastics and wood with silver. He makes gently billowing bowls and polishes the silver roughly in order to attract the light in a new way. Toward the end of the 1960s, he produced a remarkable collection of pins and necklaces in gold, using high-carat gold scales and layering them, like feathers on a wing, and further capturing the light with Mexican water opals in jewels which are at once barbarically splendid, unsettling and imaginative.

Theresia Hvorslev, who also made her debut in 1964, showed remarkable skill from the beginning. In a masterful way she makes use of all the glittering and light-catching effects of silver in jewels which are, at the same time, lively, organic and physiologically easy to wear. She has won several international diamond contests. During the last few years she has also devoted herself to larger pieces of silver—bowls, teapots and the like. She has her own smithy and sales office, The Silver Button, in Lidköping.

Bengt Liljedahl began in the strict "cylinder" style, but his style, too, has become softer, more organic, in softly pleated platters with broken or facetted surfaces. He has also created plastic rings with various color effects. He is, however, best known for his church silver.

Other names which came into prominence in the middle of the 1960s were *Owe Johansson,* who made pendants with thin silver balls in irregular forms, and *Jan Lundgren*, with platters and bottles in soft, irregular angles. He is perhaps best known for his popular, slightly battered "hip flasks," a new and amusing effect which seems very modern.

Carl Gustaf Jahnsson has, in addition to his silversmithing, also been active as an industrial designer. In his first exhibition in 1966, he displayed, among other things, church silver and tankards with an interest-

ing flattened form. He especially understands how to use concave surfaces in a way which makes apparently conventional surfaces and forms
exciting and imaginative.

Among the other silversmiths who came to attention during, and left
their mark on, the 1960s were Tre Smeder (Three Smiths) in Stockholm,
who in 1966 arranged a travelling exhibition which toured the country
for a couple of years and actively contributed to increasing interest in
new silver works. They represented rather different styles: *Claës Giertta's* vessels are boldly virile; *Rey Urban* showed proof of a versatile,
supple talent in both jewelry and decorative articles; and *Lars Fleming's*
silver pieces were made in a cultured, traditional style. Each has later
gone his own way. Claës Giertta has been involved in larger decoration
jobs, for example in the United States.

In Göteborg, Kedjemästarna (The Chain Masters), the brothers *Anders* and *Sven-Erik Högberg* and *Karl Ingemar Johansson,* have specialized in chains and links which are hardly flattering but which have fine
qualities of simplicity and strictness. *Cecilia Johansson* uses the same
cubist-functionalist language in rings and pins with geometric patterns.
Lars Arby also works in Göteborg, designing, among other things, silver
balls and other almost sculptural objects in baroque style.

Ibe Dahlquist and *Olov Barve* in Malmö used a more unusual material, bronze, in their first works, about 1962, but later turned to silver,
while retaining and developing the forms they had arrived at. Ibe Dahlquist uses thin clappers, rods and cut-off half-cylinder forms with various surfaces which she fastens together to make chains or mounts in
rows on top of one another in pendants. The medieval art of the island
of Gotland has been important as a source of inspiration for Olov
Barve's round, patterned bracelets, which are molded in sand.

It is possible to distinguish two lines in the new generation of young
silversmiths which is beginning to make itself known in the 1970s: those
who more or less are associated with the strict, pure, classical tradition,
although with a new language of form, and those who work more freely,
more romantically.

The former group includes *Nils Nisbel,* teacher at the School of Arts
and Design in Stockholm, with exquisitely hammered, well balanced

Bengt Liljedahl:
communion service
of silver for the
Tannefors Church,
Linköping, 1965.

Nils Nisbel: thin
hammered silver
bowl, 1976.

bowls in large format with leaf-thin edges, and young *Bengt Bellander,* who displays two different profiles: one more traditional and one freer and more experimental, starting, to be sure, from classical forms, but at the same time giving the objects a feeling of this era by allowing waves, cuts and reliefs to give an irregular life to the surfaces. In many of his works, even useful objects, his purpose is to create a balance among different geometric forms and volumes.

Among the romantics is *Olle Ohlsson,* who during the 1970s has more and more proved to be an original and expansive talent in silver. He works in a romantic style, influenced by nature, but also by *art nouveau.* His vases, jewels and bracelets seem almost to be organically growing, with surfaces richly ornate in a welter of forms which appeal to the eye and to the imagination. The silver is sometimes used as background for stones, forming drop-like growths, whose sheen is enhanced by the gold which Olle Ohlsson uses along with the silver. During the 1970s, his dissolving forms have been replaced by more concentrated and purer forms. Olle Ohlsson concentrates in order to be able to work the silver without using etching or the dentist's drill.

Heinz Decker also draws his inspiration from nature, decorating his vases and bowls with light, understated relief patterns.

Karlheinz Sauer in Västerås uses contrasts between gold and silver in his jewelry, often with decoration soldered on. *Bertil Kempe,* in the same city, works with simple basic forms and likes to use etching in his jewelry and larger pieces.

Something of the wild vegetation of the *art nouveau* style can be seen in *Per Arne Terrs Lundahl's* silver works, while his "chalky" pins may give associations to the oysters and mussels of the sea. He creates pendants made of silver scales or thin, glittering gold rings, and he has used colored glass from the collections of Mona Morales-Schildt in stamps and seals; with his own company, in Växjö, it has been natural for him to use glass in connection with silver.

Hannelore Dreutler in Linköping works with simple, repeated forms in her jewelry and is seriously engaged in attempts to make silver jewelry at a low cost. Elegant grace characterizes the jewelry which *Kerstin Öhlin-Lejonklou* creates in Östersund. She prefers to work in gold,

Olle Ohlsson: teapot of silver, chased, with pearwood handle, 1977.

which she hammers into thin plates or cubes in decorative necklaces and rings.

Anna-Stina Åberg in Nyköping makes, among other things, napkin rings in which she cleverly uses a monogram as decoration. *Inga Lagerwall* likes to weld her jewelry. Her form language is a rich one, alternating among soft forms, crystal-like structures and raw surfaces.

Katarina Taikon and *Bengt Janusch* are responsible for an exotic, colorful side to Swedish silversmithing. In richly decorated pieces, often in large, almost unmanageable sizes, they associate to gypsy traditions and techniques, heavy and sensual, with chains and filigree work.

Among the younger generation, *Ann Christine Hultberg* attracted

Theresia Hvorslev: "Flower of the Imagination," silver ring, 1974.

attention with her journeyman test work, a tea set in which global forms, brought together and cut off, formed an original whole. Her arm rings and rings are closed forms, sculptures in which something happens. She utilizes her thorough knowledge of the tension of the material. In addition, *Per Myrström* creates battered vase and bowl designs in silver and brass.

An important center for qualified silver during the whole of the 1960s was the silver exhibition of the Handicrafts Association (Hantverket) in Stockholm. The economic depression caused the closure of this outlet. But the Society of Contemporary Swedish Silver (Föreningen för nutida svenskt silver) has continued its pioneer work and has succeeded in furthering the interest in silver which was created during

*Kerstin Öhlin-Lejonklou:
ring in silver with precious
stone, 1975.*

*Ann Christine Hultberg:
tea service in silver, 1972.*

*Per Myrström: silver
vase, 1976.*

the 1960s. After a break, a new silver center opened in 1972 in the
Academy of Art building in Stockholm under the aegis of the Society
of Contemporary Swedish Silver, with the aim of displaying and selling
the best work done by Swedish smiths.

Continuous exhibitions and also organized travelling exhibitions give
information about what is happening in silversmithing.

In the fall of 1976, Argentum, a new gallery devoted to silver, opened
in Stockholm. Ten silversmiths, Gunnar Cyrén (who also works in
glass), Heinz Decker, Marika Dymling, Malin Gunnarson, Carl Gustaf
Jahnsson, Rolf Karlsson, Olle Ohlsson, Sigurd Persson, Karlheinz
Sauer and Martin Öhman (whose large-scale works for sacred and
profane use are marked by classical simplicity and honest seriousness),
have joined to form a company, Argentum. In addition to the obvious
goal of expanding interest in Swedish silver, the ten silversmiths want to
expand to the international market and also introduce foreign colleagues to Sweden.

Dag Widman Textiles

Modern Swedish textile arts have their roots in the handicrafts movement of the last century and the national romantic movement of the turn of the century, with its hectic artistic activity. Textile folk art—on its way to disappearance during the latter part of the 19th century as industrialism picked up speed—was the subject of an inventory at the beginning of the 20th century, under the direction of the Association for Swedish Handcrafts (Föreningen för Svensk Hemslöjd), which had been founded in 1899. At the same time a number of local handicrafts associations were formed all over the country, and in 1912 they combined into the National Association of Swedish Handcraft Societies (Svenska Hemslöjdsföreningars Riksförbund) which is still the central organization for Swedish handicrafts. Many of today's leading textile artists got their first training at a local association and in contact with living folk textile art. The palpably great interest in textiles among ordinary people in Sweden is, without a doubt, largely due to the vital handicrafts movement.

Märta Määs-Fjetterström AB

Even so, new textile arts developed partly in opposition to the traditional ideals which dominated the early handicrafts movement. The most significant textile artist for a long time was *Märta Määs-Fjetterström,* who made her debut as early as the turn of the century but who made her most important contributions during the 1920s and 1930s. In Båstad in southernmost Sweden she founded her own workshop in 1919, a workshop which became an important textile center. Märta Määs-Fjetterström created a modern Swedish form of rug art, inspired by Swedish peasant textiles and Persian rug art, but mostly by Swedish nature, the light Nordic summer. She died in 1941, but a rescue campaign succeeded in preserving her workshop and its activities for the future.

For the position of artistic leader for Märta Måås-Fjetterström AB, a workshop for Swedish rugs and woven goods, as the new institution is still called, the board was successful in getting *Barbro Nilsson*, even then well-known for large monumental tapestries, made in cooperation with various artists. Barbro Nilsson immediately engaged two students, Marianne Richter and Ann-Mari Forsberg, for the workshop and started producing new patterns along with those of Måås-Fjetterström. Over the years, Barbro Nilsson has done great things with monumental tapestries for public places and with a number of rugs which are today considered classics. With her technical skill, she has renewed older methods of weaving and made rugs that sing with color and still are in harmony with the places they are intended for.

Marianne Richter is still active with Märta Måås-Fjetterström AB. Her talent is for creating patterns with deep roots in folk art, generous and rich in imagination. In 1952, she created for the Social and Economic Council's room in the United Nations building in New York a drapery with an area of 200 square meters. In recent years she has designed new, original patterns for rugs, for example, "Korsvirke" (Cross-Timber) in a peasant technique. She has also done significant work in patterns for machine-woven rugs. *Ann-Mari Forsberg* is more sparing in her production. She has made graphically clear patterns for rugs but, especially, a series of large tapestries, all with connections to Swedish history, Swedish summer and Swedish culture. *Barbro Sprinchorn,* who died in 1973 at the age of 44, was also part of the circle of artists at Märta Måås-Fjetterström's workshop. She made her debut at the end of the 1950s with large-scale applications, combined with embroidery, clearly showing an independent talent. These formed the point of departure for compositions for tapestries characterized by free forms and picturesque imagination. After Barbro Nilsson, *Kaisa Melanton* served as artistic leader for the Märta Måås-Fjetterström AB from 1971 to 1975. During this period, among other things, she supplemented the workshop's stock of rugs with new, bold patterns. We will have reason to return to her later.

Kaisa Melanton: "Journey in Space," detail of tapestry in "röllakan" technique for the entrance hall of the Huddinge Hospital. Märta Måås-Fjetterström AB, 1971.

Gösta Werner: detail of curtain for the Skärholmen School, appliqué of spinnaker sailcloth of nylon. Handarbetets Vänner, 1974.

Märta Måås-Fjetterström's workshop employs a relatively permanent circle of artists. All the rugs are made by a group of skilful weavers in Båstad in the province of Skåne in south Sweden; some of the tapestries have also been woven in Stockholm.

Handarbetets Vänner (HV)

The center of free monumental textile art in Sweden is Handarbetets Vänner (roughly translated as the Friends of Textile Art Association and which hereafter is referred to as HV) in Stockholm. This institution was founded as early as 1874, and at the turn of the century it laid the groundwork, in cooperation with the leading artists of the time, for the free pictorial tapestries which have been so important in Swedish art in the 20th century. Between 1951—1977, the activities of HV have been led by *Edna Martin*. A talented textile artist herself, she has with great success acted as coordinator between the artists and the approximately fifteen weavers whose skill is on the highest level.

To begin with, Edna Martin hired two young, original artists for HV, Kaisa Melanton, mentioned above, and Sten Kauppi.

During the 1960s and 1970s, no less than about thirty artists have cooperated with HV. Among them are *Siri Derkert* (tapestry for the city hall of the city of Höganäs), *Eric Grate* (tapestry for the Swedish Embassy in Moscow), *Acke Oldenburg, Ingegerd Möller* (tapestry for the Blackeberg Hospital in Stockholm), *Hans Krondahl, Lennart Rodhe* (an 18-meter-long tapestry for the National Record Office in Stockholm), *Endre Nemes, Gösta Werner* and *Max Walter Svanberg*. Using Svanberg's surrealistic, oriental, colorful art, HV has made a number of important tapestries which were shown, among other places, at the Biennale for tapestries in Lausanne. One of his works is in the Hotel de Marle, the Swedish Institute's house in Paris. At HV, Edna Martin has carried out a change from weaving *haute-lisse* to *basse-lisse* (horisontal warp), which means that one can weave with the right side up.

The production of HV is intended almost entirely for public buildings.

With its experimental views and openness for new artistic solutions, the more than 100-year-old HV is today, without a doubt, one of the

most important centers in the world for producing unique textile works of art. Despite its key role, it is struggling with financial difficulties.

Individual workshops

In addition to the large workshops, Märta Måås-Fjetterström AB and HV, a great flow of textile production has taken place at a number of private individual workshops.

As early as the 1920s, *Alf Munthe* (1892—1971), originally a painter, was composing textile works for public buildings. He was for a while HV's foremost artist. From 1951 until the end of the 1960s, he

Max Walter Svanberg: detail of "Imaginary Flowering," tapestry in free gobelin technique, made in cooperation with Edna Martin, Handarbetets Vänner, 1974.

and *Greta Gahn* had their own workshop in Leksand in the central part of Sweden. His textile work, as critic Ulf Hård af Segerstad has said, is characterized by a unique mixture of refined sensibility and almost mathematical precision. He produced a number of works for churches and other public buildings which were often based on old techniques of weaving and a feeling for the room they were created for. For that reason, he became, to a high degree, an artist for architects.

An artist of importance for the decoration of Swedish public buildings is *Alice Lund*. Her tapestries, rugs and curtains are marked by skilful technique, a splendid feeling for materials, simple geometric forms and a quiet color scale inspired by impressions of nature. She has also worked for industrial production. She used to collaborate with *Sofia Widén* (who died in 1961), an artist who contributed much to the fields of church textiles and applications. *Ingrid Dessau*, who originally worked for home industries, is among the leading rug artists. With her patterns for the Kasthall rug factory, she has also contributed to the renewal of industrially manufactured rugs, primarily in the "rya" and "röllakan" techniques (the latter a type of kelimlike rug woven on an ordinary loom).

Winds of change during the 1960s

The 1950s was a rich decade for meter goods in textiles, printed or woven. The 1960s was a rich decade for unique textile art. At a large survey exhibition of Swedish art handicrafts, called Form Fantasy 1964, arranged by the Swedish Society of Industrial Design, a new generation of textile artists emerged, with a new and unconventional language of form and color.

Most of them were students of Edna Martin at the School of Arts and Design. Conscious of what they were doing, they asserted with vigor the independence of textile arts from other artistic media. Some of them neatly adapted traditional techniques to their own individual expression, while others boldly turned their backs to all tradition and revolted against it. They cut their pieces of cloth up or let yarn ends billow as from worn army banners. Edna Martin contributed to this freedom. She arranged inspiration periods, with music, exotically aromatic spices and the recitation of exciting passages from curious books. She also tried to inspire her pupils to take up the old traditional techniques, but to use them in a new way in a new language of form.

One of the students who emerged at Form Fantasy was *Helena Hernmarck*. She used a very old folk technique as a basis, a technique of patterned weaving called "rosengång" (rose path) and adapted it to what she called "free rose path."

This technique is faster than tapestry weaving, and she utilized it in early tapestries based on a rhythmic play of hieroglyphic-like expressive signs, seemingly floating in rapid movement in contrast to the static pattern of the "rose path." In the middle of the 1960s, she moved to Montreal, then lived in London and is today active in New York. Toward the end of the 1960s, she began to work with photographic material as the basis for her work. This is also in one of her most significant works of the period, "Newspapers," 1968, for the press room in the Sweden House in Stockholm. Today she weaves bold, realistic pictures for modern institutions. With her way of working she has independently

Helena Hernmarck: "Sailing," tapestry with "röllakan" base and "free rose path" top, 305 by 671 cm. For the Federal Reserve Bank of Boston, USA, 1976.

Elisabet Hasselberg-Olsson: "The Home," plucked weaving in two-leaved linen twill, 1970.

renewed the art of tapestry weaving and made an international career unparallelled by that of any other Swedish textile artist.

Two others who made their debuts at the Form Fantasy exhibition were Margareta Hallek and Maria Triller. *Margareta Hallek* previously produced flowery expressionistic tapestries but has made an original contribution with experimental textiles which activate the public by giving it, for example, the possibility of altering the appearance of the work by pressing buttons.

Maria Triller is one of the most talented weavers of her generation. More than anyone else, perhaps, she paints with the yarn and has translated impressions of Swedish nature into large tapestries with strength and integrity. Among her works is a curtain for the Hotel de Marle, the Swedish Institute's house in Paris.

The emergence of a freer style in the middle of the 1960s led to a number of joint or individual exhibitions by a number of very young artists, showing highly individual means of expression. Among these were *Agneta Flock,* who does, among other things, textile sculptures, colorful and with high spirits ("The Velvet Jungle"). *Elna Hansson* weaves pictures with motives from the world of sports or syntheses of experiences ("Venezia"), in which she often mixes various techniques, such as tapestry weaving, "rya" rug-knotting and folk methods of weaving. *Eva Schaeffer-Ek* works with large clear areas of color, often with figures as motives.

Elisabet Hasselberg-Olsson has a special position. She began weaving in the middle of the 1960s, appearing first with reserved Chinese tapestries in white or very sober colors, in which only the nubble of the woof, light as a breath, suggested a movement or a simple motive. About 1970, new realism entered into her art. She has depicted abandoned houses ("The Home," 1970), a cloud over a moor, a closed door, all simple motives but full of atmosphere. She is still fond of very quiet colors—a gray scale fading into mild blue or light earth colors.

This is realism of another kind than that already mentioned in connection with Helena Hernmark's tapestries. *Maria Adlercreutz* appeared in 1972 in an exhibition which also showed works based on pictures in the daily press. But her pictures reflect an intensively human

Maria Adlercreutz: "Like Siblings," basse-lisse, 1973.

and political involvement. Her protest against the war in Vietnam was a powerful reaction to a current situation. Her works are based on candid newspaper pictures, but her method of weaving makes her tapestry a very humane comment on a general human tragedy ("In Her Eyes the Light of the People Is Reflected," 1972).

In the middle of the 1970s, a group of textile artists appeared in Göteborg, very consciously reflecting political and social opinions in their art. One of these is *Sandra Ikse-Bergman* who, in technically skilful tapestries, often with photographs as the basis for her work, has depicted the lives of women, either factory workers in Sweden or situations from the Third World. She seeks a focal point where the trivial meets the monumental, as critic Beate Sydhoff puts it. *Gunwor Nordström* also works with themes of women quietly struggling ("Cleaning Woman"). A third artist is *Elsa Agélii,* who uses the same theme, but most often with embroidery.

The general liberation which took place during the 1960s also released new powers in some important textile artists who had made their debuts much earlier. One of them was *Ulla Schumacher-Percy,* who appeared with embroidery as early as the 1940s. During the past ten years she has come to be one of the most remarkable free textile artists in Sweden. In 1960 she displayed a series of "rya" rugs with color variations on a common pattern. A few years later she came with a series of large embroideries inspired by the buildings of the Spanish architect, Gaudí, with their organic *art nouveau* forms. During the 1970s she has, up to now, presented two mighty exhibitions. One had as its theme "The Human Landscape," in which she depicted in a number of intensive tapestries man's bondage and freedom. The other had figure-heads as a theme, in which dreams and myths about the sea and people took form. Her work is marked by strongly poetic inspiration concretized in structurally rich tapestries.

Among the really important artists is also the previously mentioned *Kaisa Melanton.* Her special characteristics appeared first about 1960, and since then she has shown the ability to renew her ideas with a number of large-scale works for, among other things, city halls, schools and prisons. Her imagination works with unexpected effects, and she experiments uninhibitedly in various techniques. But the sense of surprise and originality in her work is mostly experienced in a free, but clear and simple, form, in which color has a leading part. Melanton is also active as the chief teacher in textile arts at the State School of Arts and Design, where she has been employed since 1970 and where she is also in a position to influence today's Swedish textile arts.

There is good reason in this connection to mention *Sten Kauppi* again. He comes from northernmost Sweden. In early quick sketches in embroidery, in huge tapestries and applications, he foreshadowed the liberation in form in Swedish textile art which has already been described.

There are still other textile artists who have developed a personal language in their art. One is *Viveca Nygren* who, in colorful works, has arrived at great simplicity in almost completely white, skilfully made tapestries. Another is *Åsa Bengtsson* who has composed a num-

Gunwor Nord-ström: "Cleaning Woman," gobelin, 1975.

Ulla Schumacher-Percy: "Galanta," tapestry from the Figure-heads series, 1976.

ber of larger tapestries for public buildings, in cooperation with HV and others, and has also made splendid prints. *Lars Andréasson* is really a painter. He introduced a new type of textile art at the beginning of the 1960s. He composed pictures from pieces of woven material with the cloth applied in mosaic form or forming large, billowy sculptures, giving an apparently improvised impression, but really forming strictly composed works.

During the 1970s the Swedish countryside has returned in tapestries and in a type of atmosphere that is reminiscent of the national romantic works of the turn of the century. *Mary Moeschlin* has produced intensive depictions of this type in reserved colors. *Margareta Wilk* has reproduced, among other things, the landscapes of southern Sweden in whole, quiet compositions, using only colors made from plants in her yard.

Industrial textiles

Few countries can display such an artistically advanced textile industry as Sweden. This development began at the end of the 1920s with *Elsa Gullberg*, an organizational, technical and artistic pioneer. The influence of *Astrid Sampe* was of the greatest significance. As head of the NK Textile Studio (a subsidiary of the large department store, Nordiska Kompaniet, in Stockholm) from 1937 to 1970, she did much to develop Swedish furnishings and Swedish industrial textiles. In 1946, for example, she introduced the so-called glass cloth to Sweden. In cooperation with the Kasthall rug factory, she was responsible, in the beginning of the 1950s, for the renewal of industrially woven carpets of the Wilton type, a type which Ingrid Dessau then did so much to develop.

A few years later, the Wahlbeck rug factory also adopted a new, purposeful policy concerning modern patterns. In 1955, Astrid Sampe, working with the Almedahl factory, made innovations in the linen closets of Swedish homes, giving due notice to modern demands as regards patterns, colors and quality. She did this in cooperation with artist *Marianne Nilson* and others. In general the 1950s were a decade for new ideas in Swedish industrial textiles, and these ideas were carried out during the 1960s. A number of artists, among them *Age Faith-Ell,* contributed to this.

Printed textiles for the many

Textile prints are worth a chapter of their own. Industrially produced printed cloth had a renaissance at the end of the 1920s. About 1935, Elsa Gullberg introduced film printing, and soon there was a large production. A pattern-maker on the highest international level was *Josef*

Frank, a prominent functionalist architect from Vienna who, from 1934 until his death in 1967, was active in Sweden, associated with the Swedish Pewter Co. (Svenskt Tenn) in Stockholm (this company handles all sorts of home furnishings, not just pewter). His flowering, richly drawn patterns, which are still being manufactured, have had great influence in interior decoration in Sweden. A typical Swedish contribution in printed textiles comes from the *Jobs* family in the province of Dalarna, who started their production in the 1940s and are still going strong.

In 1954, a new wave of abstract patterns for printed textiles came. The Stobo Co. in Stockholm at that time invited a number of the abstract painters then active to make patterns for industry. The artistic leader at Stobo was *Göta Trägårdh,* who since then has herself contributed to Swedish pattern-making with a number of important patterns, often intended for public buildings, printed at Strömma; she has also done patterns for the clothing industry. In 1954, too, Astrid Sampe exhibited at NK a show called Signerad textil (Signed Textiles), to which several painters also contributed patterns.

In addition to Josef Frank, the most important pattern-maker for a long time was *Viola Gråsten.* She came originally from Finland and made her debut in Sweden with colorful "rya" rugs. Since about 1950 she has been designing patterns for printed textiles, ranging over a broader spectrum than any other pattern-maker. She has designed both geometric and figurative patterns, several of which have already become classics among Swedish printed textiles ("Hazel," "Ulmus"). Her advanced sense of color has greatly influenced the art. In 1956 she became the artistic leader at Mölnlycke AB in Göteborg, staying there until the company ceased that part of its production at the end of the 1960s. She now designs for Borås Wäfveri AB.

The vital 1970s

About 1970 came a new wave of interest in textile printing among young artists. It was typical of the times to make pictures rapidly and make them widely available at a reasonable price. There arose interest in both hand-printed textiles with individual pictures made on a limited

THE GROUP OF TEN. *Gunila Axén: "Islands," printed fabric, 1975.*

Susanne Grundell: "Seashells," printed fabric, 1975.

Carl Johan De Geer: "Flying Fish," printed fabric for KF, 1975.

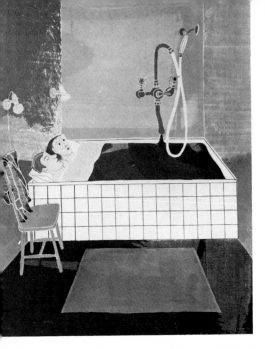

THE TEXTILE GROUP. *Petra Westermark: "We Are Drowning," her own textile print, 1975.*

Ninni Sandström: "Cornflower in Vase," her own textile print, 1974.

basis and in patterns in mass production for industry. In 1970 the so-called TIO-gruppen (The Group of Ten) was formed, consisting of Gunila Axén, Britt-Marie Christoffersson, Carl Johan De Geer, Susanne Grundell, Lotta Hagerman, Birgitta Hahn, Tom Hedqvist, Ingela Håkansson, Tage Möller and Inez Svensson (see also page 143). Together they formed a production company producing illustrations, clothes design, color schemes, etc., but the members have made their primary contribution as leading designers of printed textiles. Their patterns are often large in scale and are printed in bright colors, speaking generally, but each one has his own individual profile.

A couple of years later the so-called Textile Group was started, consisting of about forty artists working together and selling in a common

*Peter Condu: "Oppunda,"
printed fabric, 1975.*

*Astrid Sampe: "Wigg." Curtain
especially made for the main
office of the Trygg-Hansa
insurance company in Stockholm. Almedahls, 1976.*

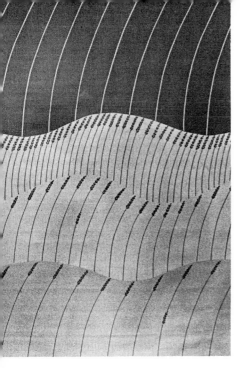

Annika Malmström: "Billowing Field." Window-shade from the collection inspired by Swedish folk music, Strömma-Sweden, 1977.

Wanja Djanaieff: "Migrating Birds." Printed fabric from the collection inspired by Swedish folk music, Strömma-Sweden, 1977.

shop in Stockholm. This group is presented in more detail on page 141.

Other print artists have chosen to work alone, for example, *Peter Condu,* who sells his prints in a shop in the Old Town in Stockholm, and *Majken Avén,* who has long been a teacher of textile printing at the School of Arts and Design.

With regard to the industrial production of printed textiles, in recent years the large deparment store chains have come to have more and more influence, such as KF Interior, IKEA and NK-Åhléns. The leading producers of these textiles are Almedahls, Borås Wäfveri and

Strömma. They work both with film printing and rouleau and rotation printing, the latter allowing rapid printing in great quantities.

Important designers who have produced patterns for these companies in recent years are Kerstin Boulogner, Louise Carling, Wanja Djanaieff, Sven Fristedt, Hedvig Hedqvist, Toni Hermansson, Hans Krondahl, Charlotte Lallerstedt, Annika Malmström, Göta Trägårdh and designers from the Group of Ten.

In industry there is also a good tradition of producing woven textiles for interior decoration of a high quality. Kinnasand and Marks-Pelle Vävare may be mentioned here as important producers with a conscious pattern policy.

Sven Fristedt: "Fructus," printed fabric for Borås Cotton Studio, 1975.

Gunila Axén: "Lion," printed fabric for KF, 1977.

Today's printed textiles extend, in pattern, across a great range—from distinct stripes and checks in a monumental scale, through traditional flower patterns and free abstractions, to primitive pictorial styles. The colors are often strong and bright. At their best, they are characterized by simplicity and freshness. This year we have seen a new interest in smaller-scale patterns and in soft and natural colors.

Summary

The Swedish textile production with artistic ambitions may, as far as the first half of the 1970s is concerned, be characterized as very vital, despite the fact that bad times have also struck the Swedish textile industry and despite the fact that the private basis for the production of exclusive, unique works has become weaker. On the other hand, this has been compensated for by the public sector, which has had an increased need of textile decoration throughout the 1960s and the beginning of the 1970s. Today it is the Swedish state, the individual municipalities and larger companies which are the largest buyers of exclusive textile art. The advantages of movability and the role of textiles in improving the environment, in contrast to concrete, glass and metal, have become obvious. Unique, individually produced work is one important pole in today's Swedish textile art. The other pole is printed textiles, which also are being used more and more in public buildings. They are also, as has been mentioned, being introduced by the larger department and chain stores all over the country, in that way reaching practically the entire Swedish public.

Barbro Petersson: "Splash, Buzz and Quack." Curtain material and furnishing fabrics, Kinnasand, 1977.

Katja Waldén Furniture

The manufacturing of furniture in Sweden has very old traditions, naturally enough in a country to a large extent covered with forests. People made what they needed themselves, but in the villages and cities there were also local carpenters who provided the communities with simple or more decorated chairs, beds, tables, sofas, in which wood was always the dominant material.

When a furniture industry gradually developed, it was concentrated in those parts of the country where usable kinds of wood were available —birch, spruce, oak, beech, among others—but where professional skills and the possibilities of transportation also were available. The furniture industry, with its center in the southern provinces of Småland, Östergötland, Västergötland and Skåne, long had the character of a small industry. In 1950, there were in Sweden more than a thousand furniture companies, and just a few years ago 600 furniture companies were employing 15,000 workers. But one single company had over 400 employees, six had more than 200, 28 more than 100—the rest were small companies with ten or so employees each.

Toward the end of the 1960s and the beginning of the 1970s, the furniture industry changed greatly. Gradually, most of the manufacture came to be done by the profitable firms, including both large and small, well-run units. The manufacturers specialize and refine their skills within a particular field in order to reach their share of the market, which has increased as a result of the demands for good environmental conditions in public buildings and at places of work. Increased exports constitute another factor.

Today there are 450 furniture companies in Sweden, including subcontractors, and they employ about 12,000 workers. There is a clear tendency toward fusions of producers in closely related industries, for example, furniture, wallpaper and flooring producers, companies in the textile, lighting and furniture industries. Large investments have been made which will probably strengthen the tendency which can already be seen, that is, the surviving companies will be, on the one hand, large companies and, on the other hand, specialized companies with profiles of their own. That is to say, they will provide products for a market wanting, on the one hand, cheap, mass-produced furniture and, on the other, expensive, hand-made pieces. It is the furniture in the medium price range that will disappear.

Production methods have been made more efficient. Some of the furniture designed in Sweden is now being manufactured in eastern-European countries, with lower production costs. Practical, easily transported packaging is a part of furniture design, and the buyer himself often must put his furniture together—all this means lower prices.

The number of furniture models, which used to be unreasonably large and individualized (it is said that 15,000 different types of furniture were on the market in Sweden at one time), has already shrunk and will surely be reduced further into fewer and more standardized types.

Rationalization on different levels has meant that Swedish furniture companies have been able to lower their prices and compete abroad. Sweden today is to a great degree a furniture-exporting country. Sweden imports a third of its furniture needs and exports just as much of its production. In figures this means that Sweden in 1975 exported furniture worth Skr 680 million and imported furniture to a value of Skr 530 million. The total Swedish production of furniture, in round numbers, was almost Skr 2,000 million.

Materials

Wood has traditionally been the major material used in Swedish furniture manufacturing. In the 1930s, in Sweden as in the rest of Europe, steel piping was introduced, and this was revived and developed further during the 1960s, along with furniture made of lightweight aluminum. In the 1950s oak and teak were the popular kinds of wood, and these were crowded out in the 1960s by exclusive jacaranda and palissander, often in veneers. The great spruce wave came in the 1970s, when spruce in robust, sometimes exaggerated, dimensions was used for beds, tables, sofas. Plastics are used mostly for furniture in public buildings, but they have found a widespread use as a material for frameworks for furniture. Synthetic materials have replaced woven cloth in upholstering, and today polyester is largely used for stuffing furniture. Presswood boards were often used in the 1960s as material for shelving, cabinets and table tops.

A new way of selling furniture

The way of selling furniture changed, too. Furniture began to be sold not only in traditional furniture shops, but also to a large extent in special furniture department stores, which displayed whole interiors and contained also every thinkable accessory for the furnishings. These are located outside larger towns, where building lots are cheap, but easily accessible to people with cars. That the buyer is responsible for transportation and also often for putting the furniture together is a prerequisite for the low prices. In 1953, IKEA opened the first environmental department store in Älmhult and since then has expanded greatly both inside Sweden and abroad. IKEA employs its own designers, and the furniture is largely manufactured abroad. The cooperative chains, KF Interior and Domus, have eight environmental department stores in Sweden, and they intend to build twenty more. KF (the Cooperative Union and Wholesale Society) which was a pioneer in cheap, good furniture in Sweden during the 1940s and 1950s, has also begun introducing measures for raising furniture quality and has begun cooperating with the Swedish Society of Industrial Design for the purpose of producing better basis furniture.

New furniture for a new way of life

The altered production of furniture of course reflects the fact that the Swedish way of life and living habits have taken on new forms. At the beginning of the 1960s, a concept of interior decoration still existed, a concept that an interior ought to contain certain definite elements. People bought, for example, whole sets of furniture, dining table, chairs and cabinet in the same style and same material.

Jan Dranger and Johan Huldt, Innovator Design, have designed, for IKEA and KF, inexpensive furniture in tubular steel or spruce. Manufacturer: Möbelmontage. Innovator's furniture and lamps at the Stockholm Furniture Fair in 1977.

"Vivaldi," 1976. Demountable armchair of tubular steel with washable cotton cover.

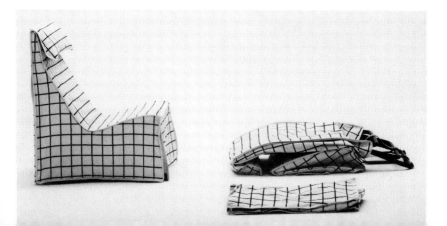

Television meant much in breaking up this stereotyped style of interior decoration. As early as the 1960s, Sweden became Europe's most televised country. Television gave Swedes new everyday habits and caused Swedish homes to be furnished differently. Comfortable groups of sofas and chairs were directed facing the television set, and tables became low tables for placing things on. "We became a population of sitters, lookers," was the way interior designer Lena Larsson expressed it.

In the next decade also of listeners; stereo sets replaced the television set as the home's foremost status object, placed in bookshelves or requiring their own space on special stereo benches. Other trends that have marked the 1970s were greater attention paid to children's furniture, greater comfort in beds and, most of all, tremendous interest in kitchens. Kitchen furniture has become more and more costly and luxurious as interest in cooking has increased.

The increasing prosperity of the 1960s also meant that more and more families could afford to have two homes, one for winter and another for summer and weekends (in itself an old tradition in Sweden). This meant two sets of furniture. The one intended for the country was simpler, lighter. The mobility accompanying the automobile—Sweden is the world's second most motorized country—also influenced furniture toward simplicity and comfort. Swedes got increased leisure time, and that meant a growing amount of simple leisure-time furniture in wood, plastics and steel. Much of it was folding, easy to transport.

The "buy-use-throw-away" mentality of the middle of the 1960s was followed by a debate, carried on with great intensity, seriously questioning the entire materialistic culture, prosperity and the so-called welfare state. This debate introduced new evaluations as to what is important and not important to have in a home. Although it was young people who most actively took part in this anti-status discussion, it reached across the boundaries of generations and gave new ideas, also to the producers. Young architects and designers designed furniture for young people without the same needs for status and durability as their parents, knock-down furniture which the handy person could put together himself, in unpretentious materials, such as pressed wood, and with robust, tough upholstery. In this field Sweden may be considered a pioneering country.

The 1970s have seen these two tendencies unite. The furniture market is offering possibilities both for the person thinking about his status and able to pay for it—a large part of this group is made up of young people—and for the person who in his furniture is seeking an expression of a simpler way of living, in which people get together, converse, listen to music, read and are satisfied with the simplest and most necessary furniture. Newly bought furniture is mixed without prejudice with older furniture, inherited or bought at auctions or used furniture shops.

Social attitudes

The development of Swedish furniture production and the success of Swedish furniture styles may be ascribed to several generations of seriously working furniture designers. A social attitude toward furniture design could be noticed as early as 1917 when the first "workers' furniture" was displayed at the Home Exhibition in Stockholm. That way of thinking has never quite been abandoned. The exhibitions of the Swedish Society of Industrial Design over the years displayed social and esthetic ideals, sometimes in sharp contrast to the commercial furniture fairs, but they gradually began to have an influence on them.

Under the aegis of the Society of Industrial Design in the 1950s there were carried out the important investigations of furniture functions, in which the quality and durability of furniture were tested in thoroughgoing trials and the results of these tests of materials were reported to aid the consumers. This activity is now being continued by the Swedish Furniture Research Institute, which is jointly financed by the Swedish government and the furniture industry. The most important achievement in the consumer information of the Institute is the labelling system, Möbelfakta (Facts of Furniture). This quality marking scheme provides easily understood information about the essential properties of the furniture.

A new initiative was taken at the Swedish Furniture Fair of 1976. In

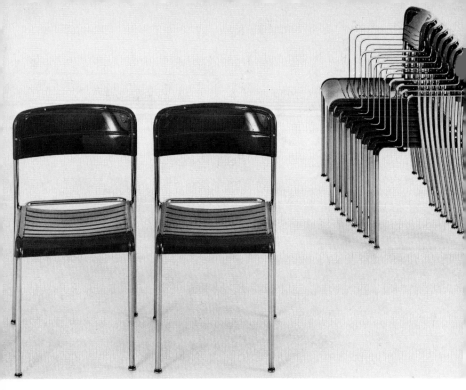

Lars Fahlsten and Lars Norinder for Åry Form AB: "Sophia," 1970. Stackable chair of chromium-plated steel with seat and back of ABS plastic. Example of one type of jury-selected furniture in 1976.

an exhibition and in a book published by the Furniture Research Institute, six experts have come up with 76 pieces of furniture (only for family use) which can be recommended, good classics and good new pieces. In 1977 an additional 135 pieces exhibiting good furniture design were selected.

Pioneers

The furniture style developed in Sweden was traditionally marked by simplicity, good usability, well thought-out design and high technical quality. Some individual designers have meant much as the source and developers of this style.

In the first place, we must mention architect *Carl Malmsten,* who used inherited Swedish skill in carpentry in designing his furniture. His furniture for the Stockholm City Hall, which became classics, is famous. During a long life (Malmsten died in 1972) he created unique hand-made pieces but also prototypes for industry. This well made, beautifully proportioned, durable and functional furniture, with a feeling of handicrafts, is still on the market.

In the 1930s, another pioneer, *G. A. Berg,* designed practical everyday furniture and demountable children's furniture in spruce and plywood, and he also further developed the Windsor chair, a traditional type of Swedish furniture.

Also in the 1930s, *Bruno Mathsson* began his research into the functions of sitting and lying down, creating new furniture forms from these measurements and demands. With rare consistency, but also heeding contemporary requirements, Bruno Mathsson has continued his designing of furniture and is today considered the leading Swedish furniture designer of the 20th century. During the 1960s, he introduced a table top in the form of a super-ellipse, held up by clamp legs, which clamped themselves onto a fastener under the table top. His chair, "Jetson," 1967, which was the first he made for the DUX company, consisted of a leather-covered steel-piping framework on a rotating steel-piping foundation on wheels. The same materials were a part of the comfortable armchair, "Karin," which has gained considerable popularity in public buildings. As upholstery for the "Karin" chair he also used the strong synthetic material, Ironside.

During the 1970s, Bruno Mathsson has designed many furniture models for public buildings, in cooperation with NK and others, and also for homes. These have included the armchair, "Birgitta," with light stuffing on a chromium-plated base, and the steel-piping bed, "Ulla," whose majestically simple form is reminiscent of the functionalism of the early 1930s. He has also presented a whole line of furniture which, in its ascetic simplicity, seems to have been inspired by Japanese design. During the whole period his early furniture in canvas and bent-

wood has been manufactured and exhibited in his showroom in Värnamo.

From the 1940s to the 1960s

In the 1940s, *C. A. Acking* designed form-pressed, stackable furniture for Bodafors, and at NK-Bo *Elias Svedberg* and *Lena Larsson* made an important contribution with their "Triva" series, simple, expandable everyday furniture, and with their healthy, unprejudiced ideas about furnishing and decoration.

In the 1950s, *Nils Strinning* introduced a new type of bookshelf, the "String" shelf, with wooden shelves placed on plastic-covered metal holders. This has subsequently been supplemented with, among other things, a table with metal legs. The same idea of expandability recurs in the "Tingotek" cabinet system which he designed for String-Seffle in

Bruno Mathsson for Dux: "Sonja," 1976. Sectional sofa of tubular steel with leather-covered cushions.

the 1970s, a light, flexible construction in beech and presswood in which a metal holder holds shelves, drawers and doors, without the necessity of screws or tools. "Tingotek" is also an interesting example of how one can use the capacity of the modern tapping machine. Nils Strinning has designed tables and chairs in steel piping, wood and form-pressed wood for Grythyttans Steel Furniture Co.

The "Sparring" and "Pira" shelving also introduced a new idea. They were constructed with supporting endpieces and consoles of steel which hold up wooden shelves and were intended to be attached to the floor and ceiling or to the wall. They could also function as room dividers. *Olle Pira* has returned in the 1970s with, among other things, the "Pira Plan" tables, benches and shelves in a light plywood construction on a steel-piping framework.

Kerstin Hörlin-Holmquist made a successful debut in the 1950s with "Paradise," a set of stuffed furniture with nicely modernized 1880-style (neo-rococo) shapes over frameworks molded in plastic. She has continued with modified traditional, well-proportioned furniture, in which the material has been nicely handled, for, among others, Karl Ruthén, Nässjö and Finnmöbel.

A fine feeling for wood and a thorough background in carpentry characterize *Karl-Erik Ekselius*, with his own company, JOC, which during the 1970s has developed a series of high-quality furniture, including "Scandinavia" in veneer, "Mondo" with an aluminum framework and leather seats in chairs and oak table tops and "Etcetera-Plus," chairs with a laminated center foot. *Alf Svensson* has designed furniture for DUX with *Folke Ohlsson* and, with *Yngvar Sandström,* designed the interesting "Form 8," an armchair with a form-molded plastic shell on a steel-piping framework, and has created excellent everyday furniture in wood for the Skaraborg Furniture Factory. *Yngve Ekström,* Svedese, as early as 1957 designed the furniture combination, "Domino," a series of low tables and chairs which became very popular for public buildings. He has been called the poet of Swedish furniture and his furniture has a touch of handicrafts, but actually is the result of consistent industrial thinking, with mountability and standardized lengths of beds and seating arrangements. Ekström's fine knowledge of

From the Stockholm Furniture Fair in 1977. Arne Norell: "Rotang," sofas of birch and rattan. Hans Ehrlin for AB Alfred Ehrlin: "Marino," shelf unit and coffee table of birch and curly-grained birch, 1975-76.

Karl-Erik Ekselius, JOC Furniture: "KS-185," 1976. Laminated chair of beech or oak with leather upholstery.

Jack Ränge for Klaesson's: "KS-298," 1977. Armchair of laminated beech, a development of Ränge's chairs from the middle of the 1960s.

Thure Liss and Lars Mossberg for Lammhults: "Base," 1976. Stackable chair in red beech.

wood shows up particularly in his fine collection of laminated bent-wood furniture for Skandi-Form, including the "Variant" series, which is also a good design for older people. Ekström's models are not affected by changing fashions and have a long life.

In the 1960s, *Hans Ehrlin* also appeared with beautiful, clean-lined furniture in light birch and curly birch for the family company, Alfred Ehrlin. In later years he has created the nicely worked-out system of shelves, "Marino," in birch and curly birch, the "Viking" series in massive spruce for Stockaryd, the steel-piping armchair, "Ricco," for the Arne Norell Furniture Co. and, together with *Mikael Björnstjerna,* the chair, "Polkett," in chromium-plated steel and duromer plastics for Overman. With *Christian Häggstam* he designed a series of chairs, tables, bookshelves and tea cart, in which the materials are chromium-plated steel and plasticized birch, for the Finnish company, Indoor.

For his own company in Aneby, *Arne Norell* designed the demountable armchair, "Scandi," in bentwood with cushions of leather or cloth, and the light safari chair, "Sirocco." After his death, his company introduced his "Ilona" model, sofa and armchair in beech with leather or cloth upholstery.

The Herbert Andersson Furniture Co. in Gärsnäs has specialized in strong, robust furniture in red beech, in production marked by practical and well thought-out details which make the individual pieces easy to care for and functional as, among other things, furniture for older people. The company hires various furniture designers for models especially suitable for red beech. *Björn Hultén* designed the "Barbro" series in laminated beech, the fine furniture designer *Åke Axelsson* made simple, attachable chairs with upholstery in linen and saddle-leather and a light, beautiful proportioned stackable armchair, and *Thure Liss* and *Lars Mossberg* designed the "LM"series, at once light and stable. These two architects have, for Lammhults, also designed a stackable Viennese chair in bent red beech, with perforated seat or covered cushion, which has every possibility of turning into a classic.

Memorable furniture types from the 1960s include *Sune Lindström's* collapsible director's chair and *Jack Ränge's* bat armchair for the Nässjö Chair Factory. Ränge has continued as an excellent and successful con-

Auditorium furnished with Jack Ränge's armchair, "KS-251," 1967, for Klaesson's. Stackable chair of laminated bent-wood beech, used in many public buildings.

structor of furniture for public buildings, manufactured by the Örebro company, Klaesson's, including expandable and attachable sofas and stackable armchairs in beech or steel with foam-rubber seats. For Gemla he has made the stackable chair, "Kaiser," in beech.

Furniture for public buildings, children and old people

Among the important designers and decorators for public buildings of the 1950s and 1960s was *Sven Kai-Larsen*, who decorated a number of hospitals and office buildings, including the Swedish Employers' Confederation's study center, Skoghem, in Lidingö, just outside Stockholm. For a special type of environment in public buildings, the office landscape, *Carl Christiansson,* along with a product group in the Facit Co., has created the "Facit 80" series. The whole series—desk, armchairs on steel-pipe bottoms, bookshelves, fiber room dividers—gives the possibility of great flexibility. Special efforts were made to allow the materials to absorb as much sound as possible. In office furniture, Formfac, with *Ralph Erskine* as designer, has also specialized in the "Combi" system.

Although the Swedish furniture industry provides well for the public buildings and home sectors (125 companies are supplying some kind of furniture for sitting), there are other special areas which are not catered to sufficiently. Only a few companies make children's furniture and only about ten, furniture for old people.

Sune Fromell was the man behind one of KF's best initiatives in the 1960s, the light, cheap and practical "Växa-med-Läxa" (Grow-and-Learn) series for children and young people. In the 1970s he has designed, among other things, "Jalusi," a series of rustic furniture for Edsbyverken, and, together with *Jan Hallberg*, sturdy furniture for Höganäs. *Stephan Gip* has designed unpretentious children's furniture with a fine sense of the child's need for gay colors, imaginative form and strong materials. He has also done the decoration of youth centers.

Good furniture for older people is manufactured by, among others, Scandi-Form, Herbert Andersson in Gärsnäs and Bjärnum's Furniture Factory, and some of Carl Malmsten's furniture is also well suited for their special needs.

Perhaps the next important area of interest in the creation of Swedish furniture will be for environments where people can get together—day-care centers, youth centers, old-age homes and informal assembly halls of various types.

The HI group, James Krenov

Toward the end of the 1960s, synthetic materials arrived in earnest, influences from Italian furniture design were strong, more exclusive types

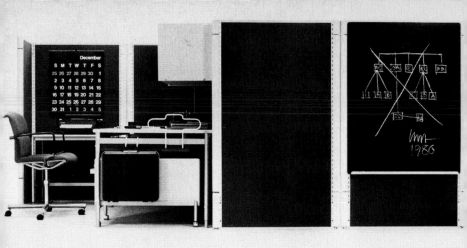

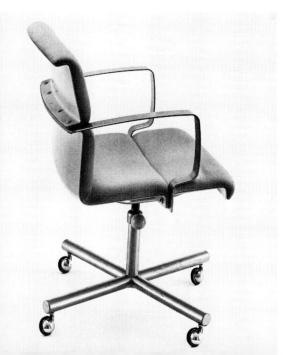

Carl Christiansson for Facit: "Facit 80," 1970. Series of furniture especially developed for office landscapes.

Carl Christiansson: adjustable work chair for the "Facit 80" series.

Sune Fromell for KF: "The Marble." Double-decker bed of spruce with storage drawers. A basic piece of furniture that has been in KF's stocks for over twenty years.

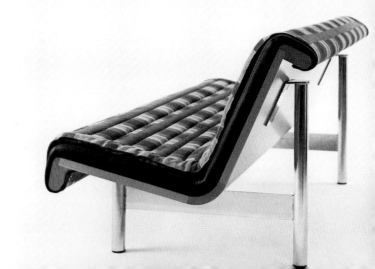

Hans Kempe and Lars Ljunglöf for Herbert Andersson in Gärsnäs: sofa of tubular steel and red beech with easily removable, washable upholstery. Specially made for waiting rooms, homes for the aged, etc.

*Music stand by
James Krenov, 1964.
An example of
superb furniture
handicrafts.*

of wood, like jacaranda, palissander and walnut, replaced teak and oak, leather became popular for upholstery. Furniture got more and more pompous, overstuffing came back, there were more and more models and constantly more imaginative ones, floors were covered with wall-to-wall carpeting. At least that was the picture at the commercial furniture fairs. It looked almost as if the high-quality Swedish furniture would be drowned in an uninhibited flow of current, worldly and international fashion trends.

But the 1960s also involved certain phenomena which had significance, at least for quality, in the development of furniture.

In 1960 the HI group was formed, an association of twelve interior designers and craftsmen. Their purpose was "to promote the exchange of ideas and personal contacts" and to experiment with hand-made furniture and prototypes for industry-made furniture. Within the HI group, *John Kandell,* along with master carpenter *David Sjölinder,* created nobly dimensioned mahogany furniture, *Lars Lönngren* and *Lars Larsson* made a series of children's furniture and *Thea Leonhard* designed storage cabinets with a simple construction for industrial production.

James Krenov is responsible for another unique contribution. Born in Alaska of Russian parents, he came to Sweden in 1947. He is something of an evangelist for wood, carefully choosing types of wood for his limited, very exclusive production of cabinets, caskets, tables and clocks. His one-of-a-kind creations should, in his own words, "appeal to calm discovery and quiet admiration, timeless things which age in a dignified, beautiful way, things with integrity . . . ."

Without exactly having formed a school, James Krenov has got successors, young lovers of wood who with intensity and sincerity adore their material and in their works bring out the character of the various types of wood, *Thomas Tempte* and *Love Malmsten. Åke Axelsson* may also be named, since he, alongside his work for industry, is also devoting himself to reconstructing, accurately and patiently, the types of furniture made in previous eras.

A new generation of furniture designers

Though the HI group and other designers mentioned above may be said to combine the views of craftsmen with openness for the demands of mass production, the new generation which appeared in the latter part of the 1960s consists practically entirely of industrial designers. They have taken direct contact with the furniture industry in order to renew production; many of them work in teams and are employed as freelancers by several different companies. It is also typical that many of them deal with design jobs along the whole scale from individual pieces of furniture to complete interiors and interior programs.

At the Furniture Fair in 1967, four students at the School of Arts and Design in Stockholm—*Jan Ahlin, Jan Dranger, Martin Eiserman* and

Cafeteria furnished with
Lammhults' tubular steel
furniture from the "S-70"
series. Design Börge Lindau
and Bo Lindekrantz, 1967.
From the municipal swimming
hall in Sollentuna outside
Stockholm.

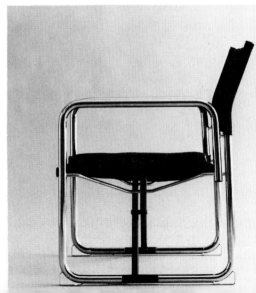

Lindau and Lindekrantz for
Lammhults: folding chair in
tubular steel in the "X-75"
series, 1973. Cushion of canvas,
self-supporting.

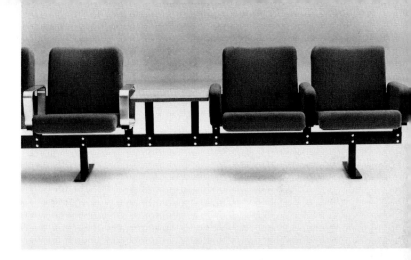

Lindau and Lindekrantz for Lammhults: the "L" series for waiting rooms, auditoriums, etc. The chairs are mounted on a steel girder and have folding seats. They come in many variants, with and without pads.

"Häcken," 1975, expandable sectional sofa. Lammhults furniture is manufactured for public buildings and maintains high quality.

Johan Huldt—presented furniture with light, movable constructions which the consumer himself could "design" to suit his varying needs. This was the foundation for a reconsideration of the "furniture concept" and an emphasis on needs, buildability and comfortable simplicity, which were to characterize the progressive part of the furniture production at the end of the 1960s and the beginning of the 1970s.

In 1968, Jan Dranger and Johan Huldt, who had founded the Innovator Design Co., displayed an interesting experiment in the "Furniture of Tomorrow" display in Tibro: a cloth covering which is filled

Göran Malmvall for Karl Andersson & Sons: cabinet from the "Svitjod" series, 1975, in birch and curly-grained birch.

Jan Ekselius for JOC: "KS-191," 1976. Stackable armchair of laminated bent beech with cloth upholstery.

with plastic foam (polyeter) which swells and in a few minutes becomes twenty times as big—inside the covering. In subsequent years, they tested various types of removable upholstery, including towelling, on steel-pipe frameworks and designed module series, manufactured from chipwood and, even cheaper, cardboard. Armchairs and sofas in this series have polyeter cushions upholstered with corduroy or blue denim. One important factor in Huldt-Dranger's design has been that the furniture has been adjusted to the demands of packaging, that is, that it is delivered in pieces for the purchaser to put together.

For KF Interior, with Möbelmontage in Enköping as manufacturer, these two designers have developed the cheap, colorful armchair, "Stuns," with heat-lacquered steel frames and polyeter-filled cushions and designed a whole furniture program, "Air-Line," which also includes lighting fixtures and textiles. It includes an armchair consisting of four inflatable tubes of laminated PVC plastic, enclosed in a sturdy, washable cover. In addition, they have designed "Woodstock" in spruce with washable textiles for KF.

In the 1970s, they have presented furniture in which the implications of their previous experiments have been developed: the "Lina" series for Viskadalens Möbelindustri with an armchair and a sectional sofa on elastic steel-pipe frames, with loose polyeter cushions and towelling coverings, and a table with a plastic-laminated top which can be raised and lowered to three different positions; steel-pipe furniture for Futura Möbler; the buildable furniture system, "Bit by Bit," in black stained plywood and with a birch armchair with polyester-covered polyeter cushions for Edsbyverken; and the "M-ETT" armchair in lacquered steel piping with canvas-covered polyeter cushions. The inventiveness and fresh ideas on furniture of the Innovators have also attracted much attention at international furniture fairs and today their furniture is sold all over the world.

Lammhults Mekaniska—Lammhults—is one of the pioneers of steel-pipe furniture in Sweden. In a pure, clean style which is reminiscent of the 1930s but which at the same time seems fully up-to-date, the team of architects, *Börge Lindau* and *Bo Lindekrantz,* has designed the "S-70" series for Lammhults: stackable chairs with a foundation of iron

Architect Carl Nyrén succeeded in creating fine interiors in the main office of the Stockholm Savings Bank in Stockholm, finished in 1975. Here the interior of the personnel restaurant, which opens on a large winter garden outside the bank hall.

piping, lacquered in bright red, blue, yellow or green. This series has been expanded with a low sofa-bed and a table with a break-top and a drawer bottom.

Their production in the 1970s includes the armchair, "Peking," in steel piping, the "PM" armchair on a steel-pipe foundation with saddle-leather cushions, a collapsible director's chair upholstered in black canvas or hemp, a folding chair in chromium-plated steel covered with woven material, a pingpong table with folding surfaces, a desk with a glued top of massive pine on a steel-pipe foundation and the expandable sofa, "Häcken," on a wooden foundation with cotton velour upholstery.

Furnishing for hotel rooms from Ruthér Möbler AB, 1977. Lindau and Lindekrantz designed this simple, expandable system of furnishing.

Bert Gutter for Sedostol: light armchair of heat-lacquered tubular steel, seat and back of natural hemp material, 1975. Can be supplemented with a footstool.

As early as 1963, Börge Lindau designed a stackable chair in beech with a form-pressed shell seat and arm supports and legs in bentwood. This model, "Opalen," has since been developed and, like many of the Lindau-Lindekrantz models, is being much used in public buildings. They have also constructed a girder system, the "L" series, in which seats, in wood with aluminum arm supports and foam-rubber cushions, are mounted on a steel girder. This exists also in a simpler variant called "Kvadrat."

For Stockaryd, *Jan Ekselius* has done a series of demountable furniture, "Alternative," with an armchair in polished oak with polyeter cushions resting on a rubber bottom, and for the family company, JOC in Vetlanda, he has designed the "Etcetera" series. This is a seat of velour-covered, 20-centimeter-thick modules of cold plastic foam, attached to steel pipes. The accompanying chair, "III," also has a chromium-plated steel-pipe foundation.

Carl-Henrik Spak works for Ulferts in Tibro, Sweden's largest furniture factory. Among his models in recent years are the "Remi" chair on a steel-pipe frame with canvas upholstery and the steel-pipe chair, "Blues," with unilon cushions.

Bo Armstrong, Bejra, has introduced a buildable series of chairs, "Attention," primarily for public buildings, with a lightweight aluminum frame holding up thin cushions. For Tua-Verken, he has designed the "800" series, tables and armchairs in dark-stained oak.

Bror Boije has had success at Plymo with, among other things, a knock-down chair and the "Wing" and "Blow" series of chairs, with washable quilted cotton upholstery. For BD-Design he has designed large-square sectional chairs and sofas with coverings of leather or linen, and light bentwood armchairs with leather and canvas seats, and for DUX the "Junker" armchair.

The great preference of the 1970s for spruce is being catered to by, among others, the Höganäs furniture company which has specialized in light, youthful and cheap spruce furniture. The company has also presented an interesting system of shelving and a large amount of garden furniture. For Fransson's in Stockaryd, *Sture Eng* has designed the "Flex" series of furniture, well proportioned cabinets, chairs and tables in spruce. Waggeryds is manufacturing the "Flora" series of shelving and the "Knagge" series of tables in natural or stained spruce, and Hilding Anders has introduced the excellent series of beds, "Polyspring," with fireproof mattress on a sturdy spruce framework. For Karl Andersson, *Göran Malmvall* has designed the well-made series of furniture, "Svitjod," in birch and curly birch.

And the future?

Swedish furniture production has been largely devoted to family living, but it is probably here that changes will be made. To be sure, people will continue to want to change their surroundings, as they always have, and right now more private one-family houses are being built in Sweden than ever before, with the demands this type of housing makes on conscious decoration.

But the big development lies in the public sector. Never before has Sweden witnessed such a boom in the construction and decorating of public buildings as during the 1970s: banks, office landscapes, personnel dining rooms, hospitals, children's day-care centers. The furniture in such places is among the best made in Sweden, and it is being ordered by knowledgeable experts and must meet special, high demands for durability, stable style, ease in maintenance and possibility of supplementing. This ever-growing part of the furniture industry is making new, difficult demands on today's and tomorrow's architects and designers—demands which ought to be able to be of use for families, too.

Swedish furniture companies will surely in the future continue to invest in product development through designers—in ever tougher competition this would seem to be vital. And if quality is to continue to involve social and esthetic considerations, the qualities which traditionally have characterized Swedish furniture design should also still be there in the future, that is to say, simplicity, usability, durability in an attractive exterior form.

Gunilla Lundahl Industrial Design

Sweden's traditionally good reputation as a country of design is based on work in industrial arts. A feeling for the tradition of form and materials was translated by artists and art craftsmen into everyday goods very early in the history of industrialism in Sweden. It was still possible to make associations with a living tradition of craftsmanship and home industry, and this was done by the idealistic associations of turn-of-the-century nationalism. The social consciousness of a small group of intellectuals and artists found a place in this and found in the Swedish Society of Industrial Design a base to use in reaching out to reality—to Swedish industry and the Swedish market.

The heavy industrialization in Sweden took place in the raw-materials field—iron, ores, wood and paper pulp. The beginnings of the flowering of the Swedish mechanical workshop industry before the turn of the century were based on Swedish inventions, such as lighthouse beacons, pumps, boring equipment, ball bearings, telephone materials —AGA, Alfa-Laval, Atlas Copco, L. M. Ericsson, etc. These still have a central place in Swedish industry. Their success has been the result of the availability of skilful engineers. Only in the last decades has design become a conceivable means of competition for them.

A first approach to entering heavy industry was made during the 1950s, with the Society of Industrial Design as the leader. The designers were still living high on their previous international successes, and the Society guaranteed good relations between designers and producers, with quality as the by-word. The motto became, "Profit by Design."

In 1957, SID, the Society of Swedish Industrial Designers (Föreningen Svenska Industridesigner), was founded. It consisted of a small, exclusive group of leading designers who watched out for their own group interests and their market, which was considered to be rather small.

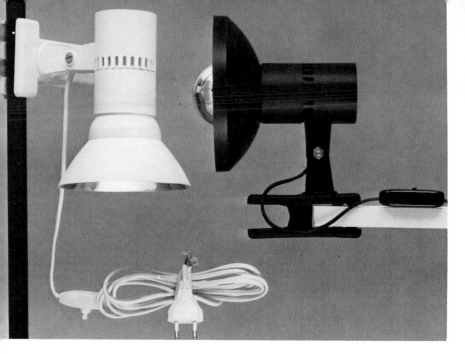

The "Fokus" lamp, AB Fagerhults, 1973. Cheap, simple spot-
light for home use. Made of
plastic with aluminium shade.
The shallow shade requires a
bulb with a silver top.

Since the middle of the 1960s,
Per Sundstedt has been designing a number of lamps which
are interesting because of their
lighting technique. The "Rikta"
working lamp, 1973, with
asymmetrical light, since 1977
in Fagerhults' stocks.

This little group had extensive international contacts, and several of them were active in the international design organization, ICSID. This meant very little to the schools of industrial design at the time. Handicrafts were their basis, and the slowly growing groups of design students were mostly involved in formal esthetic problems. Industry didn't offer them anything else, and thus contacts with industry were temporary.

The public interest was channelled via a small amount of support from the Ministry of Commerce to the Society of Industrial Design. The Federation of Swedish Industries has shown lukewarm interest in Swedish design and, before the fall of 1971, did not have anyone employed to promote contacts around industrial design.

During the latter part of the 1960s, there was growing consciousness that design is teamwork, demanding intimate cooperation at all stages of production. It became important to approach the technicians, to learn their language, but also to inform them of the work of the designer. At the end of the 1960s, SID decided to strengthen its rather weak contacts with a broad presentation at the annual Technical Fair in 1968. With a well-directed picture program, it presented ideas, working methods, the connection between products and the environment and a series of finished projects.

That same year, SID had been reorganized. Its circles were widened. The criterion for membership was made graduation from a school of art and design and further practical work. A small number of theoreticians are also members of the association. It had had a quiet existence, and it had become more and more unreasonable to deny membership to a growing group of young people who could bring new ideas to it.

At the schools, criticism grew of the training and the navel-contemplating way of looking at design. It was time for re-evaluations. In most Western industrial countries the crisis of design was obvious. The worship of technique on the part of functional esthetes was questioned. There was growing criticism of the affluent society and a growing interest in developing countries and the underprivileged.

One problem for younger designers has been to define their activity, to be able to clarify their professional role for prospective employers. Some of them find it a limitation that they can turn only to industry for

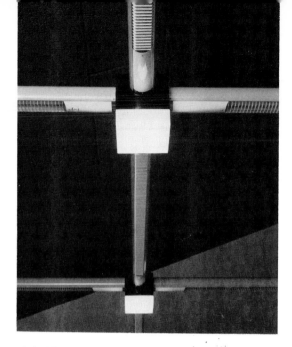

Anders Pehrson, Ateljé Lyktan, has developed his "Tube" lamps into "Tube-Combi," 1977, an expandable system for public buildings. A combination of incandescent and fluorescent lighting, which can be turned in different directions.

a job. They would like to find work in state and local administrations. Work ethics and the social role of designers are still vital subjects for debate, but, however, they have become less the center of discussion with the advent of hard times. One indication of the new ideas in this area is the number of study groups focusing on the future role of production in product development, which are being organized by SID during 1977—78.

The situation of designers

SID is still a rather small organization, although it has almost doubled its membership in the last five years, to about 180. During that time, the larger design offices were struck by crises that led to the disapperance of most of them. The largest one now in 1977 consists of the cooperating groups, the Design Group Inc. and Ergonomi Design Inc. The designers in the other offices have formed small one or two man companies or have taken jobs in industry. The downturn in the business

Peo Ström is a designer with a company of his own for lighting fixtures. Ceiling lamp in polished aluminium, part of the "Quadratic" lighting system, but can be used separately, 1977.

cycle beginning in 1973 was disastrous for the independent companies, and since then there has been no possibility of forming new ones, which means that most consultants must rely on their own limited resources.

A small number of large industries still have large design offices, although this group has not increased. Among those are Electrolux (electrical equipment); Gustavsberg (household goods of plastics and porcelain, ceramics and sanitary goods); Volvo and Saab (cars); Perstorp (plastics); Husqvarna Brush Co. (plastics and brushes) and Alfa Laval (machinery). Most industries use consultants; the most important customers are Facit (office equipment); AGA (hospital equipment, maritime beacons, electrical equipment); Philips (radio and electrical equipment); Sonab (radio and high-fidelity equipment); Solna Offset (printing equipment); the Cooperative Union and Wholesale Society, KF (furniture, lighting fixtures, textiles for the home, etc.); Ateljé Lyktan and Fagerhults' (lighting fixtures); IBM (computers); ASEA (heavy electrical equipment) and Atlas-Copco (machinery). One ten-

Lars Lallerstedt for Sonab: amplifier with receiver, "Sonab R 4000," 1971. SID's Design Award, 1974.

Christoph Egli and Hugo Lindström of the Electrolux design division design-ed "Addo 841," an electric typewriter for Facit. Design and colors compat-ible with other Addo products.

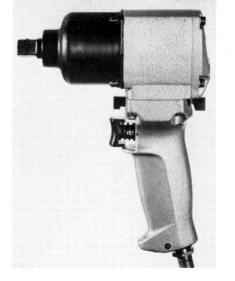

Pneumatic nut-tightener from Atlas Copco, designed by the company's design group. Robust construction, low weight, small dimensions and good ergonomic form.

Hugo Lindström, Electrolux design division, along with the company's construction engineers, designed "MHV Junior," a small industrial robot for feeding machines.

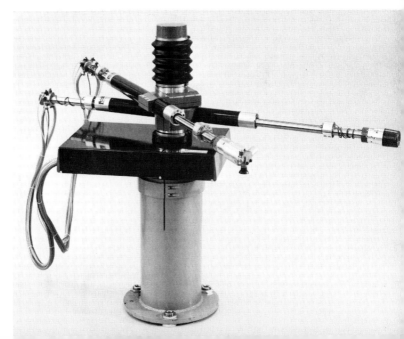

From the SID design exhibition of 1975. Two products which won Design Awards.

Automat for banknotes and credit cards for the Auto-Tank service station. Design by Kurt Ohlsson, Idéconstruction.

Atlas Copco's design group designed a transportable compressor with good muffling and good road-holding qualities when being towed. The illustration shows how the side panels can be opened to give best access for servicing.

dency found in the consumer goods industry is that it is abandoning well thought-out basis goods for those more subject to changes in fashions. This has involved moral conflicts for ambitious designers.

The situation is serious for the growing number of better and better educated industrial designers. Employment in industry provides rather a good income, but the free consultants without any organization behind them are finding their situation precarious.

There are many different principles for payment and contacts. Some companies offer set prices for the job, some work on a cost-and-profit basis within a time framework, some negotiate on royalties, and the permanently employed may have either monthly salaries or hourly wages. Some consultants make their living by working permanently with one or more companies, while others work with many different things. Some of them even start their own production when company contacts are unfavorable. SID has made no rules to be followed, but many consultants negotiate according to the rules which the interior designers have made for their organization.

SID activities

Thus reads one of SID's by-laws: "The aim of the Society is to work for the development of industrial design, to spread knowledge about it and to look after the interests of the designers."

Conferences

In order to watch over the interests of designers and spread information, it has dealt with the following factors, among others: Is design profitable? That was the name of a conference among designers and entrepreneurs in February 1972, arranged by the Federation of Swedish Industries (in cooperation with SID and the Swedish Society of Industrial Design). The marketing aspects are still the gate through which designers get into unwilling industries. Contacts have been cool for a while, but this time there was such great interest that a number of industries had to be put on the waiting list. The conference gave important space to value analysis, which has become a powerful idea in the debate on design. Using the methods of value analysis, it is easier to make esthetic aspects more understandable and to place the designer's ambition on a scale for determining its weight.

"The risk of giving the designer too much responsibility is that the functional aspects will be over-emphasized," said one of the company managers. The importance of bringing design work in at a leading level was emphasized even more by other industrialists, who gave examples of how the quality of design was responsible for their success.

SID, which was the co-sponsor of the conference, came with designers on a broad front and with greatly varying experience in industry in order to convince the industrialists of the importance of their work—heavy industrial products, light consumers' goods, graphic design and design manuals. The conference was a success, and a broader area of contact between industry and designers has been secured.

Similar informational conferences on a smaller scale were arranged in Värnamo in 1975 and as a part of the experimental work of the Industrial Board in 1976—77.

Industrial consultation

The National Industrial Board in 1975 started experimental activities with information on industrial design to small and medium large enterprises. Informational meetings were arranged in two counties with the entrepreneurs' associations, on a trial basis. This experimental activity will be evaluated in the fall of 1977, and after that the Ministry of Industry will decide how state aid to industrial design is to be given. SID members have taken active part by giving information about their work. In some cases this has led to new contacts and new working opportunities. Short informational meetings and courses with various industrial associations have also been held.

Design awards

In 1974 and 1975 SID's Design Awards were made to those companies who had produced praiseworthy products in cooperation with industrial designers. The companies have often felt flattered, but the products chosen have in some cases been criticized for not working properly. The exhibitions of the recipients of the Design Awards have not led to any

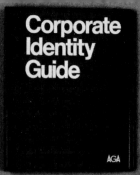

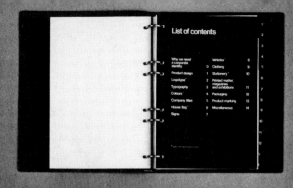

The Design Group for AGA: "Corporate Identity Guide," SID's Design Award, 1974. AGA has subsidiary companies in 28 countries. The guide contains guidelines and instructions on how the logotype and the house color should be applied to products, packaging, printed matter, vehicles, etc.

more intimate contact with the public and many designers feel the emphasis on commercialism to be wrong. In 1976 no SID Design Awards were made, and the continuation of the awards is being discussed.

Three design offices

In order to illustrate the practical realities faced by independent design offices, three representative offices have been chosen, two larger ones and a smaller one.

Designgruppen AB (The Design Group Inc.) was founded in 1969 by six designers and an administrator on the basis of collective ownership. It owns a large building in a Stockholm suburb. This building contains a carpentry shop, a mounting hall, a mechanical shop and a spray-painting room on the bottom floor, a drawing office, a library and a conference room on the intermediate floor, and a photographic studio and

The Design Group for Solna Offset: four-color offset roller press. Since 1965, the Design Group has been working with developing Solna Offset's printing presses and has made ergonomic studies of the operator's work with the press. Signs, symbols, regulators and levers have been re-designed and improved.

office space on the top floor. The designers have a broad repertory from interior design, graphic art, design of consumers' goods to producers' goods and mechanical products. In addition, they hire consultants and have some permanent employees. To a large extent they choose their own customers by visiting them. Each project has a project leader with the possibility of delegating to others. The archive and systematization work is important. The company tries to put part of the profits into free research in order to find new ways of working. Decisions are made collectively at weekly meetings. Two of the six designers opened an office of their own in 1972.

Among the company's employers have been AGA (a design manual, medical equipment, etc.); Solna Offset and NOHAB (printing equipment) and C. E. Johansson (measuring apparatus and other jobs). It has also worked with printing presses, forestry machinery and pumps. Most of the designers are organizationally active.

The company went through a critical period at the beginning of the 1970s but survived, partly because the designers could collectively make personal sacrifices and partly because they had an established circle of customers in the producer-goods industry, which was not as subject to the adverse effects of the business cycle. They now share an office building and exchange services with Ergonomi Design AB. Together they can offer apprenticeships to students. They receive many study visits and, thanks to their large model workshop, can receive customers during longer periods of discussion and study. Their office now consists of 15 members.

Ergonomi Design AB (Ergonomy Design Inc.), formerly Product Program AB, is a cooperative office, which was organized in 1970 and works together with the Designgruppen. Working with direct industrial jobs in the beginning, the company is now working to 80 or 90% with projects it has initiated itself; these projects have been financed by the Swedish Board for Technical Development, the Swedish Work Environment Fund, the Institute for the Handicapped or the Folksam insurance company. Its principal fields of activity are the working environment and handicap and hospital care. It has carried out projects on protective clothing; development of the working area for arc-welding,

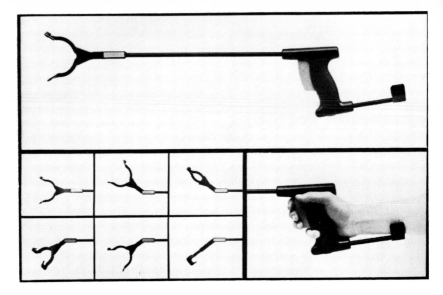

P. O. Bjurling and Sven-Eric Juhlin, Ergonomy Design, designed these grip tongs manufactured by Gustavsberg. They were developed for people with limited reaching ability, and they have a very flexible grip. The handle enables work to be done with a straight wrist. SID's Design Award, 1974.

Maria Benktzon and Sven-Eric Juhlin, Ergonomy Design, for Gustavsberg: kitchen knife with supportive cutting board, 1974. Developed specially for people with limited arm and hand functions, but can also be an improvement for people with normal functions. The knife was designed with the same type of grip as a carpenter's saw. This grip has the advantage of keeping the wrist straight and requires only a push-and-pull movement for operation. The supportive cutting board is intended for people with grave handicaps. SID's Design Award, 1975.

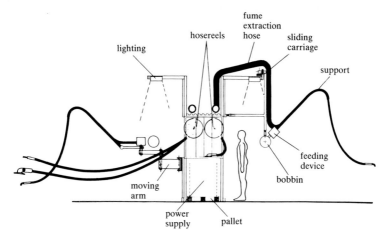

Ergonomy Design has studied working conditions for manual electrical welding. This work was done with a group of welders, and a workshop was built up in a plant. The drawings show proposals for work sites where four modules have been brought together into one unit containing everything the welder needs. The unit is covered with noise-absorbers and is equipped with lighting. The compressed-air tubes are rolled up on hosereels so as not to get in way of the worker and so as to facilitate cleaning. The welding equipment is placed on a sliding carriage which can be moved from side to side. Smoke from the welding is drawn out through the welding gun.

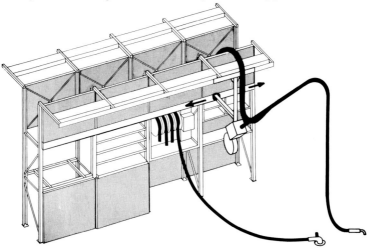

grinding and assemblage; development of tools and handgrips for the handicapped; eating and drinking utensils for persons with limited hand-arm function, etc.

The aims of Ergonomi Design and Designgruppen are these:

To work in projects for socially useful technology and thus try to include a total view on the society's production from, among others, the point of view of energy use.

To allow the demands and points of view arising from the users' situation to be the point of departure for development work in projects.

To work in problem areas where practical solutions were previously lacking or where existing products do not fill humanitarian demands that the user has the right to make.

That the result of the work should always be a concrete, practically usable solution, which should either be intended for mass production or in some other way be generally applicable.

To cooperate with manufacturing industries in pushing project proposals through the stages of planning and adjustment to production down to the final products ready for the market.

The Swedish society's great emphasis on the working environment, which started early in the 1970s, has involved expanded opportunities for working for designers who have social usefulness on their programs. The same thing is true of the increasing emphasis on helping the handicapped to lead independent lives.

The third company is *Ahlström & Ehrich Design AB*, a small two-man company, relatively newly organized, specializing both in the consumer-goods industry and in design which government officials commission.

A & E Design is an office for industrial design and product development, begun in 1968 by two young designers, *Tom Ahlström* and *Hans Ehrich*. They have their own workshop for the production of models and prototypes and work, for example, with the transportation of patients, bathing facilities for patients, queuing systems, brushes and

Tom Ahlström and Hans Ehrich,
A & E Design, for AB Turnomatic:
queue-number automat. The machine
is a development of a patented queue-
ticket machine by Åke Ehrlund. An
old model with 46 components is re-
placed by this new machine with six
injection-moulded parts. Ticket re-
loading is simplified, and the bracket
holding the machine allows it to
swivel. The new design has maximal
durability and is cheaper in produc-
tion than its predecessor. SID's Design
Award, 1974.

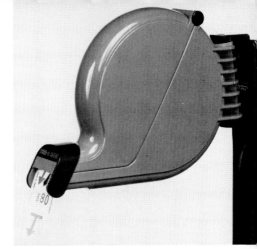

A & E Design for the Norwegian
Jordan company: scouring brush, 1975.

painting equipment, dishwashing brushes, equipment for the handicapped, lighting fixtures, furniture and interior design, packaging and graphic design.

They look upon their work in this way: "We see it as our job to contribute to the development of industrial products with a high degree of functionalism. This means that we attempt to meet the demands of both the consumer (functionalism, ergonomics, durability, appearance) and the manufacturer (adjustment to production, economy), just as we also try to satisfy the wants of distributors and sellers.

"Our products are characterized to a large extent by a strictly geometric design. We definitely turn our backs on imitations of materials, decorations and other effects, so-called 'styling,' that do not contribute toward improving a product's functional qualities."

The debate

The debate about things, their form, function and social content, is very quiet. The word, design, took on a bad sound in the 1950s when the design names were used as advertising slogans. For most people, design stands for unnecessary status thinking and sales tricks. Increased sales is also the argument the designer has, for the most part, to motivate his work, although most people seek anonymity and instead try to work for the company's profile.

The focal point of the debate on design is the Swedish Society of Industrial Design (Föreningen Svensk Form), in Stockholm, with a subsidiary and a Form/Design Center in Malmö, the only permanent exhibition hall for industrial design in Sweden. The Society's means of keeping the debate alive are the *FORM magazine,* exhibitions, debates, conferences and both internal and external contacts. An intensification of the discussion in the circles most affected has been achieved in recent years, while the general social debate, however, ignored the question of the use and value of things. There has been a noticeable swing in opinion, however, in connection with the interest in achieving a society which is more saving of natural resources. That the internal debate is lively means a preparedness to meet the growing interest in these questions.

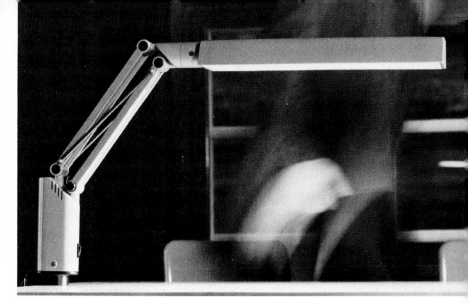

A & E Design for Fagerhults: "Lucifer," 1975-76. Neon-tube lighting fixture for work table, can swivel or be locked, manufactured entirely of plastics. In addition to the clamp foot, also comes with table or floor bases.

Rune Monö for A. H. Andersson & Co.: Thermostat mixer for the "AHA Adam" series of fixtures, consisting of basic elements and five special units — for kitchen counter, washbowl, bidet, shower and bathtub. Can be regulated with one hand and has markings for the blind.

Jan Landqvist and Sven Eklund for AB Gustavsberg: thermostat mixer, 1973-75. Part of a complete program for all sanitation units. The design of the handles is the result of functional studies; the mixer can also be maneuvered by the elbow.

Sven-Eric Juhlin for Gustavsberg: plate for school lunchrooms and plastic table setting, 1974-75. Plates of melamine plastic have room for knife and fork, mug, and food, so that trays are not needed. Easy to carry, stack, wash and dry. SID's Design Award, 1975.

The Society of Industrial Design has in recent years expanded its network of contacts abroad through, for example, exhibitions with the other Nordic countries in Australia, Brazil, Mexico, Israel and Poland. Exhibitions devoted entirely to Swedish design have been arranged in Australia, Japan and China. An exhibition on the theme "Design for the handicapped" is touring Eastern Europe in 1977.

New training on the way

Constant changes are taking place in education. A decisive and permanent change was carried out at the School of Design in Göteborg in the fall of 1971 in the metals and plastics department, which is responsible for training in industrial design. Theory has been given considerably greater room. Students are no longer bound to their materials and are given the chance to solve complex problems. It is the method and not the object which is the primary thing. Other subjects added to the curricula are: social science (including sociology, psychology and industrial economics); the environment (including homes, the working environment and city planning); value analysis; ergonomy; the techniques of presentation; design methods. Great attention is also paid to materials and production techniques so as to give the students sufficient technical knowledge to be able to talk to technicians in their own language. The new ideas were tried out the first year in a joint project on one problem: new systems of transportation.

This is an attempt to set up university-level training according to the principles of the report of the Artists' Education Commission (see also the chapter, "The Design Schools"). To be sure, the students have varying backgrounds—engineering training, basic school plus a great deal of practical experience or university training in the humanities—which gives uneven prerequisites, but which makes teamwork profitable. This in itself is no hindrance for firmer, more goal-directed training on the advanced level. A greater problem is the present mixture of handicrafts training and training in industrial design, which leads to fuzziness in goals. For the school year 1972—73, the department worked out the following goals:

"The training, which covers four years, has as its aims to:
give the students knowledge about the collaboration of human beings with products and the environment;
train the students to master general methods of solving design problems, both individually and in groups;
train the students to foresee various side-effects in a product;
develop and deepen the students' creative ability;
develop and deepen the students' abilities in visual and verbal expression;
train cooperation with representatives of other professions, for example, in project groups."

Traditionally, contacts between designers and technicians have been very weak. An attempt at getting them together started in 1968. At that time, the professor of machine construction at the College of Technology in Stockholm was invited to act as a bridge by assisting in certain exercises and helping to create the preconditions for common project work. Since then a few common projects have been tried, with varying degrees of success. The most palpable result was a garbage truck made as an examination work at the State School of Arts and Design in 1970, for which students at the College of Technology were responsible for the construction.

Another attempt to break into new work forms in the schools was the examination work done by a team of two students at the State School of Arts and Design in 1972. For a long time they were investigating ambulance transportation in Sweden in the hope of being able to persuade the half-national and half-local organizations, which are responsible for the products in this field, to change their way of thinking.

Their point of departure was to work with the whole system of transporting sick people, to show how all the functions are connected, and then to choose one product from the system, the stretcher, to give it a more relevant function. This work was one of the most consistent and well carried-out attempts at influencing and demonstrating that design has a function in administration.

Although Swedish industrial design is faced with many question marks, there are many signs that a broader and more meaningful activity is on the way, at the same time as training in design is being broadened.

During years of investigations about training in design, the idea of a school outside of Stockholm and Göteborg has often been presented. A firm proposal from an investigating commission came in 1976. A design college was proposed for Luleå in the far north of Sweden, in connection with the mining, iron and steel industries which were expanding there. The design college was to be closely integrated into the newly established college of technology and was to give the possibility for both basic training and advanced training for designers, architects and technicians. The training was to be organized around projects and on the needs and conditions of the region. (See also the chapter "The Design Schools.")

Kerstin Wickman The Design Schools

Konstfackskolan

The Swedish State School of Arts and Design in Stockholm is more than 130 years old. It was started in 1844 by Nils Månsson Mandelgren, who then founded the Swedish Society of Industrial Design as a support for the school. Mandelgren took the initiative for the school because he feared that, when the craft-guild system was abandoned in 1846, Swedish skills in handicrafts would disappear. Sweden, he feared, would quickly be flooded with poorly manufactured foreign factory goods. The school, then, was primarily a vocational school and it was given the name of the Handicrafts School in Stockholm. In 1945, the school was given its present form and name, Konstfackskolan. Since 1977 it is financed by the state through the National Board for Universities and Colleges, but also has support from the municipality of Stockholm.

The State School of Arts and Design has four courses: (1) A two-year day course in industrial art, and a three-year evening school in industrial art, both of which give a general basic education; (2) a two-year advanced course in industrial art; (3) a one-year preparatory course for art teachers; and (4) a three-year course for art education, in which all the art teachers in Sweden are trained. The day and evening schools in industrial art are the prerequisites for those who want to go on with advanced work in industrial art.

There are seven departments: metal and industrial design; textiles; ceramics and glass; furniture and interior design; advertising and graphic design; sculpture; pictorial art and the environment. About 1,000 students study at the school, approximately 300 of whom are in the Institute for Art Teachers' Training.

Acceptance at the School of Arts and Design is mostly dependent upon the work samples submitted and the results of the entrance exami-

KONSTFACKSKOLAN.
From the graduating students' exhibition in the spring of 1976:

Ulla Carlsson, Textiles Department: "Harvesting Woman," tapestry in two parts.

The Ceramics Department also teaches glass design, with practical work in glass works. Large glass platter by Claes-Göran Tinbäck.

nation. A further requirement is that one has "artistic talent and the other prerequisites for the occupation the training is for." Between 400 and 500 people apply for entrance into the art-industry departments every year, and 90 are admitted. Certain departments have, in addition, special courses to which people may apply separately. The Institute for Art Teachers' Training has room for 72 new pupils a year, and it has between 500 and 600 applications. Among the most popular departments are those for furniture and interior design and for textiles. Most people apply for the pictorial art and environment department. The average age of the students is between 22 and 23.

Before the students begin at the school, most of them must go through special preparatory courses in, for example, the techniques of woodworking and metalworking industries, bricklaying, house painting, technical work in the textile industry and techniques in ceramics and glass making. Only students who have been accepted by the State School of Arts and Design in Stockholm or the School of Design in Göteborg may take part in these courses.

The State School of Arts and Design has a good reputation abroad. Many inquiries come in from students abroad who want to take its courses. About thirty foreign students are there today.

The school is in a position to accept only a very limited number of foreign (special) students and only for one year of *advanced studies*. As a general requirement the applicants must have passed a school of equivalent level abroad*. Applications for admission must be sent in during the month of April and should include: curriculum vitae, copies of school diplomas or records awarded to the applicant, certificates from professional practice, recommendations and 15—20 slides showing his own works.

Konstindustriskolan

The School of Industrial Design in Göteborg was started by the Göteborg Society of Crafts and Design. Today it is financed by state grants

* Information on courses and requirements can be obtained from: Konstfackskolan, P.O. Box 27117, S-102 52 Stockholm, Sweden.

KONSTINDUSTRI-SKOLAN.

From the student exhibition, 1977: Ragnar Lundgren exhibited proposals for a series of furniture with reclining chair, chair, table, and bench. The reclining chair can also be extended into a bed. The series in wood is intended mostly for outdoor use.

Danaxel Lindberg and Gunnar Apelgren, Industrial Design Department: prototype for a child's tricycle. It is broader and more robust than the ordinary tricycle and consists of a few, easily exchangeable parts.

and a certain amount of municipal support. The municipality of Göteborg, however, has questioned its economic involvement in the school (all the costs except the teachers' salaries are paid by the state). In July 1977, the state took over responsibility for the school when it became a college.

The School of Industrial Design has a four-year day course with five courses of study. It has no training in decorative painting or sculpture and no training of art teachers, as the School of Arts and Design in Stockholm has. Associated with the School of Industrial Design in Göteborg, however, is an advanced graphics course.

During the past few years, the school has been adjusting to the model proposed by KUS (a state commission on artists' education), that is, to divide up the training into five courses of study with new names: product design I (hard design), product design II (soft design—textiles and ceramics), environmental design, informational design and art handicrafts, in which the students work with different materials. The school has also introduced a basic course common for all the students in the first year in which they are allowed to try out various materials and fields in order to find out what studies they want to choose during the three following years.

In the past few years, interesting projects have been carried out, especially in the department of metals and plastics. Under the heading of product design, it has been possible to take up both ergonomic and ecological questions in connection with design. Many of the projects are carried out in cooperation with companies and institutions, and the school has been able to make use of the fact that several of Sweden's heavy industries are located in the Göteborg area.

Today the school has about 450 students, but when it becomes a college and the courses of study are concentrated as mentioned above, that number will be reduced to about 220. There will be possibilities for people outside the school to supplement their training at the school with courses in certain subjects, for example color and form. It is estimated that there will be about twenty such extra students per year.*

* Further information can be obtained from: Konstindustriskolan, Kristinelundsgatan 6—8, S-411 37 Göteborg, Sweden.

An attempt to break the isolation of the design schools

In 1967—68 a wave of interest in environmental problems washed over Sweden. Suddenly there was an interest in how reality works. Work sites, hospitals, schools, school yards, the playgrounds of children in new suburbs, the possibilities of handicapped people to get along outside in housing projects, the motorized society—all these began to be discussed.

In addition, very little of what was exhibited as examination works at the design schools had any connection with what interior and industrial designers traditionally work with. Instead the students threw themselves into ideological debates and worked on broad subjects such as downtown service functions in the center of towns, construction modules for housing, housing landscapes for extended families. With the proposals were often presented thick compendia, the students' own investigations, with sociological facts, statistics, background analyses, quotations, references to professional literature and the investigations of others.

But most of all, the students discussed and debated at the schools. It was necessary for them to make clear what they wanted. They demanded responsibility for their own education, that representatives of the students should take part in the administration, that they should have influence over curricula and textbooks and over decisions that affected their own education. They were anti-individualistic and preferred to work anonymously in groups.

The future of the design schools the object of investigative commissions

In 1967 a state investigative commission, the Artists' Education Commission (abbreviated KUS in Swedish), was appointed to investigate education at the colleges of art. Its area of competence was extended in 1968 to cover the design schools, too. In the fall of 1970, the commission made its report. Although it had arrived at a number of concrete ideas which were positively received by many people, the report was met by a great deal of skepticism. The criticism came especially from the students at the School of Arts and Design and the Academy of

Art, who were of the opinion that the need for "artistic education" in society and the role it plays in society has not been investigated sufficiently. They also objected to KUS' proposal of attaching training in art handicrafts to the colleges of art.

Between 1967 and 1971 came a change among the groups of students who were active and dominant at the schools. During the late 1960s it was the future interior designers and industrial designers. Later the pupils in the pictorial art and environment department began to be significant for the schools.

In 1967 and 1968, the debate about whether handicrafts were to continue or not was intensive. Art handicrafts almost became an "immoral employment, since all it did was to provide the upper classes with luxury articles." In later years, when ecological consciousness has produced suspicion of industry, handicrafts have become a more environmentally acceptable form of production and have won in strength. Similarly those pupils who want to learn art handicrafts. The increase is remarkable.

The proposal of KUS was, briefly, as follows. The state commission proposed five "form colleges" for a broad basic training and three design colleges and three art colleges for more specialized education.

One of the ideas behind the five form colleges was that the training should be spread throughout the country instead of, as now, being concentrated in Stockholm and Göteborg. But after the debate about KUS, many people questioned whether the society's need for artistically trained people really was as great as KUS had reported. Many of the students leaving the schools of design are now having trouble getting jobs.

In 1973 a new state commission on artistic training, called K73, was appointed, and it has published two partial reports. In 1974 it made a proposal concerning "questions of the organization of studies in the fields of pictorial art, art handicrafts and design." In 1976 it reported its views on how many people should be trained at the School of Arts and Design and at the Academy of Art, with proposals about the continued training and supplemental training of those active in the fields of pictorial art and design.

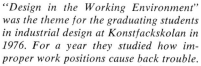
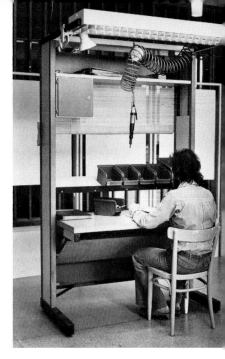

"Design in the Working Environment" was the theme for the graduating students in industrial design at Konstfackskolan in 1976. For a year they studied how improper work positions cause back trouble.

Håkan Bergkvist and Hans Himbert designed a flexible workbench for assembly line work. The height of the workbench is infinitely regulatable, giving the possibility of a variety of working positions.

The School of Arts and Design may plan its training in detail

Several large state commissions have dealt, from different points of departure, with questions of the education of future art craftsmen and designers over the past ten years. There is still no definitive proposal as to how training at the School of Arts and Design is to be organized.

At the moment there is at the School of Arts and Design a division into three specialties—design, art handicrafts and free artistic expression. The Minister of Education, in his summary of the reactions to the

K73 report, emphasized that "the need for artistic expression and the fine artistic work of the students themselves must not be endangered . . ." And "free work with picture and form and independent artistic depiction are a common part of education which must be particularly emphasized."

The proposal of maintaining a department for artistic training at the school, then, would not involve competition with or a reproduction of the comparable training given at the College of Art. Free artistic training at the School of Arts and Design should be aimed at jobs giving form to the environment. This has in later years taken place in practice, in work on ecological and social problems.

But what is lacking today is sufficient contact with the society outside the school—although much effort has been made in recent years to attack real problems in society and jobs that touch on the pupils' future work.

What is required is that the present organizational structure for this activity be altered so that certain workshops in the school become independent and thus available to all the students. In addition there should be workshops with specialized equipment.

Since the fall of 1974, the School of Arts and Design has been given the economic resources for and the possibility of carrying out a certain amount of experimental activity with projects and seminars across the boundaries of specialties. It is hoped that this work will lead to the development of new courses of study.

On many points, K73 is a continuation of KUS. However, K73 recommends giving the basic training for the two schools—the one for free art and the one for design and art handicrafts—the possibility of having their own profiles. According to KUS, this basic training would be the same for both. In the latest proposal, the point of departure would be a common plan for training. But the basic training should be given at the same school where the student will later specialize. Upon being accepted, the student must immediately choose which course he wants to follow. There would be possibilities for changing, however, after the basic training.

During the basic training, the student should be able to try out various

"Design in the Working Environment," Industrial Design Department at Konstfackskolan in 1976. Johan Dahlberg and Stig Gauffin studied work with air-pressure drills. In order to eliminate improper pressure on parts of the body, take away the vibration and lower the noise level, they proposed a stand to lighten the work of drilling and cutting.

materials and techniques at the same time as he takes a preparatory course for the specialized course to follow.

The most important and interesting part of KUS' proposal was that the basic training should be open, not only for those students who intended to specialize as art craftsmen or designers, but also for future journalists, architects, etc. K73 also considers that several professional groups would find it useful to have such training and should be able to get credit for it.

The basic training is to last two years. After the basic training, the training would be divided into the following courses: environmental design, product design, informational design and art handicrafts; in the art handicrafts field, there would still be specialties, such as textiles, metalworking, etc. Including the basic training, the course would last a total of five years.

The students' examination jobs in the field of the working environment dominated at the Industrial Design Department at Konstfackskolan in 1977, too. There were proposals for improvements in trucks. Per Forssell worked on designing instruments and levers for maneuvering dolly trucks. He systematized functions, put all signal lights on one panel, put the buttons in a group by themselves and the maneuvering levers in another.

The School of Arts and Design to become a college

But it is not just these two commissions that have touched on the future of the School of Arts and Design. In 1975, the Organizational Committee for the Stockholm Region of Higher Education, H75-S, presented an extensive proposal for including the School of Arts and Design among the other college units in Stockholm. The School was, together with the Dramatic Institute, the College of Art and five other colleges in the field of art, to be a part of a special institution, the "College for Artistic Training." The Institute for Art Education, however, was to be moved to the "College for Teacher Training."

Exactly how the situation will be in the future has not yet been determined. Many of the schools are afraid of being deprived of the freedom they have, in spite of everything, to plan their training.

A new kind of industrial designer

The working environment—especially the environment of heavy industry—is an area in which designers may make many contributions. But that requires qualified knowledge of ergonomy and another type of technical training than that the art industrial schools now can provide.

For that reason, another state investigative commission has proposed that design training should be included in the training of civil engineers now being done at the College of Luleå. That course already includes studies of machine technology and labor science, and the idea is that it would be natural to integrate these with advanced artistic education, with the working environment as the point of departure. The course would last five years, with a two-year basic training course in common for the three proposed major design courses: working environment, product design and informational design. The commission also points out the need the northern part of Sweden has for such education. There are several heavy industries there. The commission has suggested that fifteen students per year be accepted for each course.

Some time in 1978, the authorities will make a decision about this commission's proposal.

Kerstin Wickman Work Situation and Social Commitment

The work situation

One hundred and fifty students are accepted, in hard competition, for training in the art industry schools every year. After graduation, they find the competition no less hard. Many have difficulties finding jobs in the household goods industry. The situation for interior designers, who have had an especially hard time in the 1970s, brightened somewhat in 1976. More jobs have awaited them.

Because of the new law on security of employment, many companies are disinclined to hire new people. For that reason, it is getting more and more common for interior designers and other designers to work as free-lancers, often two, three or four together. There are also some large offices in which several designers share space and resources.

Handicrafts making a comeback

Toward the end of the 1960s, the status of handicrafts had reached bottom. Instead of working with objects, art craftsmen were to go out as teachers of amateurs and in social-welfare surroundings, among children and the handicapped.

But at the beginning of the 1970s, conditions changed. Interest in art craftmanship has grown stronger and stronger. This has meant, among other things, that courses which were considered things of the past at the School of Arts and Design have suddenly begun to be in demand again among students. For example, about ten students in the department of graphic design have been taking a course in the art and techniques of bookbinding.

Also in other fields, interest in handicrafts has increased noticeably. For several years, there were no students specializing in silversmithing. But at the student exhibition in 1976, a whole class appeared with im-

Interior of the textile department of the Collective Workshop in Stockholm. Textile artist Åsa Bengtsson, of the Textile Group, works with silk-screen printing of her own textile print, "Marble Horse."

pressive silver objects, both jewelry and useful objects, produced with really time-consuming handicrafts methods. The metalworking department has in recent years been divided up into two departments, one specializing in industrial design and the other one devoted to silversmithing.

In the sculpture department, journeyman tests have been taken in ironmongering, and many students have made their own, very well made, tools. The crafts techniques have also returned to the glass and ceramics departments.

Many of the students graduating with craftsmen's training have been starting their own or sharing workshops.

All the extensive investigations and large projects, often socially oriented, which were so usual at the end of the 1960s are now completely lacking.

This does not mean that all the ideas that appeared at the end of the 1960s have been abandoned. Many craftsmen are working with pedagogical activity. Many are also trying to achieve their results together with those who are to use them, based on the needs of the consumers. And among craftsmen a mutual solidarity has arisen which has led to the situation in which groups no longer work only for their own purposes but also for those of their colleagues.

Unity gives strength

This has meant that many of them have joined together, either to solve the problem of making contact with buyers and sales channels or to facilitate experiments and production on their own. An example of this latter course is the textile division of *Kollektiva verkstan* (The Collective Workshop) which is located in an old former factory building at Rosenlundsgatan 29 in south Stockholm. Since the fall of 1970, its members have had access to fantastic technical equipment. One can become a member by paying Skr 300, and one can use the machinery for about Skr 20 a day.

To get this activity started, the state invested Skr 150,000 and the municipality of Stockholm made certain guarantees. As its basic equipment, the textile division bought a print table, silk-screen equipment, dyeing vats, engraving vats, drying and development ovens, a mangle, rinsing vats, washing machines, a spin drier, two different kinds of looms, warps, bobbins, etc.

Since 1976 it has also had a dyeing plant and has been sharing a large monumental workshop with other workshops. In it, the artists can try out large curtains and tapestries. Other studios do not have that possibility.

In addition to the textile division, there is an enamel workshop, a ceramics workshop, a plastics workshop, a glass workshop, a hall for

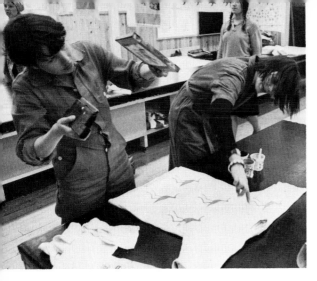

From the Textile Workshop in Umeå in northern Sweden. It was previously also open to the general public on certain evenings, and now study circles are held, sponsored by adult education organizations.

The sales and exhibition rooms of the Textile Group on St. Paulsgatan in south Stockholm. Separate exhibitions are arranged here regularly, and there is a collection of slides showing work by the members.

sculpture and general exhibitions, a smithy, a mechanical workshop, a photographic division, a lacquering division and, since 1976, a bronze and graphic division. The workshops have a total area of 1,800 square meters which 450 members share. They take time about taking care of the place. A board of ten persons has been elected by the members.

The workshop received about Skr 40,000 from the state, through the Cultural Council, for the latest investments. The members themselves paid for the rest.

The municipality of Stockholm subsidizes the activity with about Skr 130,000 a year, which is the amount of the working deficit.

Smaller collective workshops, supported by the state and the local governments, exist in several places in the country.

Here, then, there are great possibilities for experimenting with various techniques, a freedom that a private textile artist can seldom afford. Those who have worked together at the textile division realized that the problems that they thought were individual problems, primarily the difficulties in finding buyers for their products, are shared by others. Thus, they have been able to put up a broader front and to arrange actions.

In 1973, about forty designers and craftsmen joined together to form the *Textile Group Inc.*, an economic association which obtained a common shop in order to get direct contact with customers and "break the traditional pattern of profiteering middle-men." The showroom and shop are at St. Paulsgatan 5 in Stockholm.

The members work with different textile techniques. The shop offers hand-printed goods by the meter, one-of-a-kind pictorial tapestries, cloth collages and one-of-a-kind prints. There is also a file of slides showing examples of the works of the various members.

The shop is planned in such a way that everyone will have the possibility of displaying his or her textiles during the year. There is a special room for these separate exhibitions, and a timetable on which the members can sign up for when they want their exhibitions. The daily keeping of the shop is done by the members themselves taking time about. This means that each member must take the responsibility for sales and other activity for two weeks every year. The members have a

The first textile collection of the Group of Ten was displayed at two exhibitions in Stockholm in the fall of 1972.

The permanent showroom of the Group of Ten on Gamla Brogatan in Stockholm contains fabrics for sale. In 1974 the members of the group exhibited five new patterns.

full meeting once a month, and they are divided up into four interest groups: one managing the practical work concerned with the shop, the exhibitions, etc.; one working to improve the working conditions of the members; one group working on ideas; and a fourth dealing with public relations.

Otherwise all the members work individually and are responsible themselves for the presentation of their own works in the shop. There is, for example, no jury for choosing works to be displayed.

Each member pays Skr 40 a year, and ten per cent of all sales in the shop goes into the common treasury. This is five per cent if it is a matter of acting as go-between in a commission.

With the years, the Textile Group has become well known. This means that its members have not just got a channel to reach the consumers. It has also given them the opportunity of making contacts with interior designers and manufacturers. Thus they have been invited collectively to make textile decorations for the IBM laboratory in Lidingö, for the new hospital in Sundsvall, etc. They have had group exhibitions in, for example, the United States and at the Nordic Council's cultural center in Reykjavik, Iceland, in addition to smaller exhibitions in libraries, schools and hospitals.

Some of the members have cooperated in making common designs for a collection for a French company. Several designers making patterns together—patterns based on collective expression—would have been considered impossible a few years ago.

But another group of textile artists had already proved that that was possible. This was the *TIO-gruppen* (The Group of Ten Inc.) which began working together as early as 1970. Their motives were partly different from those of the Textile Group. The Group of Ten consists of designers all of whom had had experience in working in the textile industry. But they found that they had difficulties in carrying out the ideas that they themselves wanted to.

The Group of Ten has a shop at Gamla Brogatan 32 in Stockholm which the members take time about in running. They share profits alike, regardless of whose patterns sell best. Still another motivation for beginning their cooperation was that they wanted to counteract thinking of textiles in terms of fashions, that is, removing a pattern from stocks after one season and bringing in another one. Good patterns must have a longer life, they insist.

The Group of Ten has exhibited its printed fabrics in Paris, New York, Helsinki, at the Sweden House in Stockholm and at Form/Design Center in Malmö. They have also made the textiles for decorating several government agencies: the National Administration of Shipping and Navigation and the new care centers of the National Prison and Probation Administration in Eskilstuna and Saltängen in Norrköping.

The textile designers in particular, 99 per cent of whom are women, have begun many new working forms and unconventional solutions. One such is the newly founded *Swedish Design Bureau*. It also consists of four textile artists with many years of professional experience and a broad background both as clothes designers, interior designers, pattern designers, etc. They are Kerstin Boulogner, Wanja Djanaieff, Boel Matzner and Aino Östergren. Nytorgsgatan 7 in south Stockholm is the address of their office, combined with a sales and exhibition hall called The Bureau Drawer. A workshop will also be attached to the office, since they intend to manage the whole work of product development themselves with, for example, sample garments. A collection of clothes for children and men is in the works, as well as textiles for interior decoration, etc.

The Clothing Group is a less formal grouping, consisting of textile artists who have specialized in clothing for handicapped people.

In Swedish textile factories, it is difficult for artists to make ends meet. Designers often have little opportunity of seeing to it that their patterns and the final results turn into what they had intended. Colors are changed, shadings erased, etc. Many textile artists have, in vain, insisted for years that the designer should constantly be present in product development. The textile industry is often marked by a fear of investing in bold, "new" patterns.

Today the Swedish textile industry is undergoing a crisis. Considering the low working wages abroad, its products are finding the competition more and more difficult. "For that reason it is more important than ever for us to stick together and develop new forms for training and new ways of working," said the textile designers working in industry.

In 1973 they organized the *Association of Swedish Textile and Clothing Designers* (usually abbreviated STOK), with about 170 members active in industry. The Association's aim was to "create insight into our responsibility to the consumer, the environment and the society."

The Association holds regular meetings twice a year. In between, small groups meet, working around certain subject-matter fields (seven in all) or on a local basis. Thus there are groups in Stockholm, Borås and Göteborg.

It used to be a matter of being individually strong in asking for pay for a pattern. Now the artists have STOK to support them. Thus the members of the payments group have worked out payment norms and basic contracts, etc.

The education group is to organize advanced training courses and to answer requests from government investigative commissions for opinions on educational matters.

One way of spreading knowledge and aims is to hold exhibitions. At an exhibition of textile prints at the Cultural House in Stockholm in 1975, the STOK group presented a division showing the working situation of the textile designers and the course of their work from sketch to finished cloth.

The working group for cooperation wants to strengthen contacts with similar organizations in the design field for cooperation on professional and legal questions.

The program must be based on reality, and for that reason there is a special group, the crisis group, which collects the experience of members concerning work conflicts in order to find out why and when cooperation between designer and producer does not function. And in it perhaps STOK has its greatest psychological significance for a professional group whose members mostly work entirely alone or alone in groups with other categories of workers in industry.

STOK has become a very useful organization for the designers. Here they find people who understand what they are talking about, what they are working for and who share their experience. They find security in one another. It is not a matter of star designers defending their own positions but of helping to create a good atmosphere for more jobs, equal conditions, just payment and better products.

The Program Group Inc.—nine interior designers

Interior designers have also organized themselves into groups. The *Program Group Inc.* started in 1968 and became a collective office, collectively owned, in 1973. All its members graduated from the School of Arts and Design between 1966 and 1971, worked together on examination jobs and during their period in the school made contacts which gave them the possibility of continuing to work, for example, the examination job of the proposal of making a new office building in Stockholm into a service building with exhibition halls, rest rooms, a café, a post office, telephones, etc., as a balancing factor to the more and more commercialized center of town. That is, a place where people might meet without its costing anything. What this project was to contain was just then being debated. The building was never made into a service building. But the municipality of Stockholm was so interested in the project, anyway, that it employed the group for another large-scale project. This involved the welfare bureaus or social-service centers which were to be decentralized and built in various housing projects in the Stockholm area. Thirteen have now been built out of a total of eighteen planned.

These new welfare bureaus will contain, in addition to the old welfare offices, bureaus for child care, for the care of alcoholics, for children's day care centers and for domestic services to those who for some time need help, e.g., retired persons. This means a concentration of social aid institutions in one place. Today the various bureaus are housed in several different places, which means a lack of contact among them, and that visitors must often travel great distances from one to another.

The Program Group wants to put further activities in the new welfare bureaus than just those which have to do with social and economic problems, so that other people will also come to them. They think it is important to dedramatize the welfare offices so that people who go there will not need to feel that they are social failures. By putting all the bureaus in the same building, it will be possible to coordinate the need for space and instead invest the money and space saved in such a way as to make the environment more comfortable in this building, which they would prefer to call a citizens' center, rather than a social welfare bureau.

But the group has not worked just with welfare bureaus and other jobs of interior design. It has also organized exhibitions for the home-consultants, a non-commercial activity which spreads information about food, clothing and furnishings, etc., national exhibitions and information about handicapped people to the public, for example, an exhibition about the problems of the mentally retarded. It has also designed anti-smoking campaigns, a comic book published in 250,000 copies about the problem of sniffing thinner and study materials.

Ceramic artists organize

A group which has been formed with the Textile Group as its model is *Blås & knåda* (Blow & Knead) at Köpmantorget 1 in Stockholm's Old Town. In the summer of 1975, 23 ceramists and glass designers with their own workshops opened a common shop. Working there gives the artists direct contact with their customers. Discussions about quality, needs, professional roles, etc., are also organized there.

There are economic reasons for such cooperation. The artists can make joint purchases of clay and other materials, cutting out middle men and keeping prices down. Through the shop, all of the members have increased their annual incomes and sold more than they ever did before.

And this is needed—for, in spite of the fact that the public interest in art handicrafts has increased during the 1970s, art craftsmen form the professional group in society that earns least.

In Göteborg, art craftsmen worked to get a building where they could have their workshops and various kinds of activities. It is today called *Konsthantverkshuset* (The Handicraft House) and it is in the Haga district. And in other cities there are centers for art craftsmen and other so-called cultural workers—for example the *Designhuset* (The

Design Building) in Lidköping, where the noted ceramist, Carl-Harry Stålhane, former artistic director at the Rörstrand porcelain company, has started a ceramic workshop and cultural center.

Kulturrådet

Kulturrådet (the Cultural Council) is the government institution which, among other things, works for art craftsmen, that is, it awards grants for individual works and projects and arranges exhibitions so that the works can be spread to larger audiences. This year, 1977, for example, a state grant of Skr 2 million has been proposed for the decoration of people's parks and other assembly halls. This may give work to many pictorial artists. The Cultural Council also gives financial support to many of the collective workshops and is preparing a proposal to give artists and art craftsmen grants for exhibitions. Beginning July 1, 1977, the Swedish Society of Industrial Design will also receive its yearly state grant from the Cultural Council.

A new view of the environment

The great interest in environmental questions at the end of the 1960s was particularly concerned with the social environment, the problems of underprivileged groups and how one could achieve an opener society in which people of various ages and from various categories might meet. This was a protest against children segregated in day care centers because of age, housing projects for university students only and old people and the handicapped isolated from the rest of society.

There were also objections to centralization, which involved over-population in the big cities and the impoverishment and depopulation of the countryside. A number of young people moved out to collectives in the countryside in order to grow their own food and live in a healthier way, in which work and leisure time were in harmony with nature.

The Association of Göteborg's Art Craftsmen is responsible for the Handicraft House that opened in 1974 on Skolgatan in the Haga district in Göteborg. The building contains sales and showrooms and workshops.

The ARARAT exhibition at the Museum of Modern Art in Stockholm in 1976 exhibited alternative solutions for energy use and for a society with better balance between man and nature.

House heated by solar energy.

A wind generator is being set up.

A group of architecture students built a "recycled" house out of surplus materials.

The pollution of natural resources, spraying food with poisons, industry inimical to the environment are obvious threats to the future.

Handicrafts began to be taken up again as a form of production less dangerous to the environment and one using less energy, in which one could control both the process and the end result. This has led the pupils and teachers in the art industrial schools to take up in their instruction ecological questions, and projects to solve ecological problems and inter-disciplinary seminars on ecology have been carried out. The schools give the students and teachers the opportunity of making experiments for which there is no room in industry.

There are a number of environmental groups working with various aspects of environmental questions, food, nature, production, energy questions—all from the point of view of ecology. Some of these presented a large-scale exhibition at the Museum of Modern Art in Stockholm in the summer of 1976. ARARAT was its name, and it was built up by artists, designers, architects, technicians, specialists in the humanities, craftsmen and students at the School of Arts and Design in Stockholm and the School of Design in Göteborg.

The exhibition attempted to show lines of development for a future low-energy society, in which nature and human beings lived in balance and products were manufactured with and operated by solar, wind and water power. There were low-energy systems of food preservation and preparation, buildings heated by solar energy and run by energy from wind masts, etc. The center of the exhibition depicted natural cycles and flows. There were products made from reusable materials and examples of techniques used in developing countries. During the whole course of the exhibition, seminars on energy and production were held. "Health, Durability and Beauty" was the motto of the exhibition. This expresses a new attitude, in opposition to that of the society of superfluous consumption.

The discussion on quality is now being carried on on many levels. It is not just about having products that last a long time but also about making them of natural materials (a protest against plastics and synthetic fibers) and about a form of production that is not dangerous either for those who work in the manufacturing or for nature.

Facts on Societies, Museums and Exhibitions

Föreningen Svensk Form

Föreningen Svensk Form, former Svenska Slöjdföreningen (The Swedish Society of Industrial Design), is a nonprofit organization supported by the state Government. Founded as early as 1845, it is one of the world's oldest organizations of its kind. The Society has a total of about 7,000 members who are supporting the Society by subscriptions to *FORM* magazine. The Society consists of three special sections; the designers' section with about 250 active designers and specialized journalists; the manufacturers' section which consists of leading factories and companies associated with design and architecture; the consumers' section consisting of educational, women's, and consumer organizations and public utility building enterprises. The board is composed of three representatives from each section and six members elected at the annual meeting.

The statutes indicate the aim of the Society as "to further good design of Swedish products, to work for better private and public buildings and environment, to spread information on good design." The Society is engaged in practical activities as well as in influencing public opinion.

Form/Design Center at Lilla Torg in Malmö is an independent institution run by the southern section of the Society.

The Society is also responsible for temporary exhibitions in Sweden and abroad. Since 1974 the Society has arranged design exhibitions during the summer months at Galleri Heland at Kungsträdgården, Stockholm. Swedish design exhibitions have been shown in Japan 1972, in Australia 1975—76 and in China 1976. Scandinavian industrial design exhibitions have been touring Brazil and Mexico in 1970—72 and Israel and Poland in 1974—75.

FORM magazine (The Swedish Design Review) gives information and debates problems concerning design and environment. *FORM* follows the developments in the field of industrial and interior design, art handicraft and public environment in Sweden as well as abroad. *FORM* appears with eight issues a year. Subscribers abroad receive a special edition with a summary in English.

The Expert Body of the Swedish Society of Industrial Design gives opinions on matters of copyright infringement and design protection. It is composed of ten experts on industrial design who have been elected by the board and is presided over by a jurist.

Conferences, courses and debates are organized by the Society and are important activities influencing public opinion.

The Society runs an important contact and information activity. It composes programs for foreign researchers, specialized journalists, designers and buyers. It arranges visits to industries and workshops. By way of its archives the Society supplies photographs to foreign magazines and lecturers.

FORM magazine as well as general information can be obtained from Föreningen Svensk Form.

Office: Nybrogatan 7, telephone +46 8 63 59 20

P.O. Box 7047, S-103 82 Stockholm.

Form/Design Center, Lilla Torg, telephone +46 40 10 36 10

P.O. Box 4309, S-203 14 Malmö.

Föreningen Svenska Industridesigner

Föreningen Svenska Industridesigner, SID (The Society of Swedish Industrial Designers) has about 175 members.

See pages 103—113.

Office: Malmskillnadsgatan 48 A, telephone +46 8 14 20 00

P.O. Box 1419, S-111 84 Stockholm.

Föreningen Sveriges Konsthantverkare och Industriformgivare

The Association of Swedish Art Craftsmen and Industrial Designers (called KIF in Swedish) was formed in 1961 as a nonpolitical professional organization for art craftsmen and industrial designers. At present it has about 300 members.

The right to get grants for exhibitions and not to have to charge value-added taxes for their works are two of the questions that KIF has been working on in recent years.
Office: Nytorgsg. 17 A, S-116 22 Stockholm, telephone +46 8 44 05 20

STOK
The Association of Swedish Textile and Clothing Designers has about 170 members. See page 145.
Office: Odengatan 3, S-114 24 Stockholm, telephone +46 8 24 02 30

Svenska Inredningsarkitekters Riksförbund
Svenska Inredningsarkitekters Riksförbund, SIR (The National Association of Swedish Interior Designers) originated in 1933 as a nonprofit union. Currently, the aim of the organization is to inform the public of its members' qualifications for the purpose of benefiting society as well as the individual. In addition the association is working to improve the profession and to promote trade interests among its members. The members of SIR (currently numbering 580) are interior designers educated in Sweden's two schools of design. The Association publishes *Forum Närmiljö,* a magazine for its members.
Office: Odengatan 3, S-114 24 Stockholm, telephone +46 8 24 02 30

Museums and exhibitions
Argentum, Hamngatan 6, Stockholm, a new showroom for modern Swedish silver.
Form/Design Center, Lilla Torg, Malmö, was started in 1964 and is administered by the Swedish Society of Industrial Design. Form/Design Center is a permanent exhibition of a selection of furniture, textiles, light fittings, glass and china on the market and a temporary exhibition activity on current topics. The Design Center also serves as a locality for common use with a great variety of activities such as a workshop, debates, film evenings, club activities, etc.
Föreningen för Nutida Svenskt Silver (The Society of Contemporary Swedish Silver), Jakobsgatan 27, Stockholm, a permanent exhibition of contemporary Swedish silver.

Konsthantverkarna (The Society of Swedish Craftsmen) is an organization of about 200 practising artist-craftsmen throughout the country. Konsthantverkarna has a retail sales room in Stockholm (Mäster Samuelsgatan 2) which is also the organization's office.

Kulturhuset (The House of Culture), Sergels Torg 3, Stockholm arranges temporary exhibitions of art handicrafts and design in the department "Konsthantverket" on the 3rd floor.

Nationalmuseum (The National Museum of Fine Arts) in Stockholm contains the country's most distinguished collection of modern Swedish art handicraft and art industry. A new department of industrial design is being planned. The development during the first decades of the 20th century can be studied in this representative selection. The Museum also arranges temporary displays of modern Swedish design.

Röhsska Konstslöjdmuseet (The Roehss Museum of Arts and Crafts) in Göteborg is the only special museum in Sweden for applied art. It includes a rich collection of modern Swedish art handicrafts and it presents frequently changing exhibitions of modern Swedish design.

Svensk Möbelcenter Furniture Mart AB, Storängsvägen 10, Stockholm, is a permanent exhibition of 26 manufacturers of furniture, light fittings and textiles.

In addition there are showrooms and department stores, mainly in Stockholm, Göteborg and Malmö showing Swedish design. The Swedish Society of Industrial Design publishes the annual designguides *Scandinavian Design in Stockholm, Gothenburg and Malmö* with addresses of department stores, showrooms and design shops. The folders can be obtained from the Society of Industrial Design.

Bibliography

Beard, Geoffrey, *Modern Ceramics*. London 1969. 167 p. (15 p. on Sweden.) Studio Vista.

Hård af Segerstad, Ulf, *Scandinavian Design*. Stockholm 1961. 130 p. Nordisk Rotogravyr.

Hård af Segerstad, Ulf, *Modern Scandinavian Furniture*. Stockholm 1963. 131 p. Nordisk Rotogravyr.

Hård af Segerstad, Ulf, *Keramik. Sekelskifte till sjuttiotal*. Stockholm 1976. 32 p. Text in Swedish, 109 pictures. Rörstrand.

Klyvare, Berndt, Widman, Dag, *Stig Lindberg—Swedish Artist and Designer*. Stockholm 1962. Rabén & Sjögren.

Krenov, James, *A Cabinetmaker's Notebook*. New York 1976. 200 p. Van Nostrand Reinhold Company.

Lundgren, Tyra, *Märta Måås-Fjetterström och vävverkstaden i Båstad*. Stockholm 1968. 119 p. Summary and picture captions in English. Bonniers.

Nylén, Anna-Maja, *Swedish Handicraft*. Lund 1976. 428 p. Håkan Olssons.

Stavenow, Åke, Huldt, Åke H (editors), *Design in Sweden*. Stockholm 1961. 269 p. Bokförlaget Gothia.

Widman, Dag (editor), *Svenskt konsthantverk från sekelskifte till sextiotal*. Yearbook from the Swedish National Museum of Fine Arts. Stockholm 1967. 158 p. Summary and picture captions in English. Rabén & Sjögren.

Willcox, Donald J., *New Design in Ceramics; New Design in Jewelry; New Design in Stitchery; New Design in Weaving; New Design in Wood*. New York 1970. 120 p. per volume. Van Nostrand Reinhold Company.

Zahle, Erik (editor), *Scandinavian Domestic Design*. Copenhagen 1961. 300 p. Hassings Förlag.

Exhibition Catalogues

Design in Scandinavia. Exhibition catalogue with text by Ulf Hård af Segerstad. Stockholm 1968. 70 p. Svenska Slöjdföreningen.

Nordisk Industridesign. Exhibition catalogue with text in Swedish, English and Finnish by Alf Bøe. Göteborg 1971. 56 p. Röhsska Konstslöjdmuseet.

Adventure in Swedish Glass. 16 artists from Kosta-Boda and Orrefors. Exhibition catalogue with text by Helena Lutteman. Perth 1975. 76 p. The Swedish Society of Industrial Design.

Gustavsberg 150 år. Exhibition catalogue with summary in English. Stockholm 1975. 84 p. The Swedish National Museum of Fine Arts.

SID's Design Award 1974. Exhibition catalogue with text in Swedish and English. Stockholm 1974. 72 p. The Society of Swedish Industrial Designers.

Svensk industridesign 1975. SID's Design Award 1975. Exhibition catalogue with text only in Swedish. Stockholm 1975. 63 p. The Society of Swedish Industrial Designers.

Swedish Textile Art—Five Temperaments. Exhibition catalogue with text in English and Spanish by Beate Sydhoff. Malmö 1976. 28 p. The Swedish Institute.

Design Reviews

Kontur (Swedish Design Annual) Nos. 1—13. Stockholm 1950—1966. The Swedish Society of Industrial Design.

FORM magazine/The Swedish Design Review. Summaries in English. Published eight times a year by the Swedish Society of Industrial Design.

INTERIÖR (Swedish Interior) review with Swedish furniture and interior design with text in Swedish, English, French and German. Published twice a year by Möbelindustrins Service AB.

Index of Persons